100 Ways
in 100 Days to
Teach Your Baby
MATHS

Matador
9 Priory Business Park,
Wistow Road, Kibworth Beauchamp,
Leicestershire. LE8 0RX
Tel: 0116 279 2299
Email: books@troubador.co.uk
Web: www.troubador.co.uk/matador
Twitter: @matadorbooks

ISBN 978 1800464 490

British Library Cataloguing in Publication Data.
A catalogue record for this book is available from the British Library.

Printed and bound by CPI Group (UK) Ltd, Croydon, CR0 4YY

Matador is an imprint of Troubador Publishing Ltd

For Henry and Isla,
who have taught me more
than I could ever teach them.

EMMA L SMITH ACA FIA

100 Ways
in 100 Days to
Teach Your Baby
MATHS

Support All Areas of
Your Baby's Development by
Nurturing a Love of Maths

Edited by Barbara McNichol

CONTENTS

"*The strongest predictors of later achievement are school-entry math, reading, and attention skills... early math skills have the greatest predictive power, followed by reading skills and then attention.*"

– GREG DUNCAN,

Professor of Education, University of California

PREFACE

Some people enjoy mathematics, and their confidence in this area helps them with many aspects of their life—from small everyday decisions to significant areas such as the career paths available to them.

They are the lucky ones.

But is it really luck? Are some people genetically predisposed to understand numbers and others not?

It is not uncommon for people to casually state they are not good at maths. This admission seems to be acceptable in a way that would not be if they struggled with basic literacy. Why is this? What impact does it have on their children?

When researching dyscalculia—defined as a "severe difficulty in making arithmetical calculations"—sadly, it did not surprise me to discover that one category of dyscalculia included this quotation:

> "A parent may have said something along the lines of 'I could never do maths at school and it never harmed me'. While such statements may well have been made with the best intent, they can, in many cases, undermine any subsequent attempt to help the young person overcome difficulties with maths."

– TONY ATTWOOD, founder, The Dyscalculia Centre

For me, this comment highlighted the important role that we, as parents or carers, have in assisting our children to feel confident about having a go at maths. Confidence can lead to enjoyment. In turn, enjoyment can allow children to fully embrace this important area as they maximise their ability and future opportunities.

I felt it was important for the cycle of maths anxiety to be broken. What better way to do that than by surrounding babies with the language of maths via books, nursery rhymes, toys, and activities. This familiarity would help them on many levels. They would not be nervous when encountering maths in formal education. In addition, they would build a secure and strong bond with their parent(s) through the one-to-one time invested—and their literacy skills would improve, too. I could see no downside.

It was a significant moment when I stumbled across a study by Professor Susan Levine. Her study confirmed my assumption that infants who heard more "number" words went on to achieve better maths results in school. How simple. How easy. How sad that many babies miss the opportunity to maximise their maths ability because this fact is not widely known.

From here, I investigated as many "baby maths" studies as I could. The hard evidence was so compelling, I wanted to share it with you in this book.

The evidence kept reinforcing these key points:

1. Babies seem to be born with an amazing number sense: understanding shapes in the womb, being aware of quantities at seven hours old, assessing probability at six months old, and comprehending addition and subtraction at nine months old.

2. The best time to introduce maths is infancy. By the time children enter school, there is already a significant gap in maths skills.

3. A parent's attitude shapes a child's attitude. You have the power to teach your baby that maths is enjoyable and not something to be anxious about.
4. Your baby can learn maths while boosting all other areas of development. For example, movement will be boosted while teaching geometry positional language, literacy will be boosted while reading a "number" book, and bonding will be boosted while giving your baby your undivided attention teaching maths to him or her.
5. Babies will use maths every day for the rest of their lives. That's why maths is important.

This book has no worksheets or tests, and the activities can fit in with busy days. By providing hints, tips, and suggestions to engage with your baby about maths, it breaks down this huge subject into 100 easily digestible topics. Every day for 100 days, you will find an activity, song, or story that helps introduce your baby to maths. Notice which activities work well for your baby and highlight the ones that resonate with you. Determine those that motivate you to continue teaching your baby maths and, by doing so, encourage all areas of development.

Most of all, this book provides evidence to help you realise how amazing your baby is as you get to know his or her potential to embrace numeracy from birth.

FOREWORD

For many centuries, there has been an argument raging. It goes like this: "Is maths a natural part of the universe, or is it an idea invented by people?" Put another way, "If we ever discover aliens, would they 'do maths'?"

Here's a second question: "Are people who just don't seem to understand maths suffering from a genetic malfunction or just bad schooling?"

A lot of people have spent a huge amount of time arguing about these questions. And occasionally, I've been invited to join in. When that happens, I can be rather awkward and raise another question: "What number do we have in our maths that doesn't exist in Roman numerals?"

I ask this to show that maths itself can be an exploration.

So, what about this missing Roman number? A bit odd, isn't it? After all, the Romans ruled much of Europe, Britain, and North Africa for 2000 years. How could they have missed out a number? What did they do—go "one, two, three, five…"?

In many countries, maths is considered to be dull. And of course, some people find maths really, really hard. Some even say they just can't do it. Indeed, some poor souls—those we call dyscalculic—don't get maths at all. They are not just poor at maths; they really can't do it at all.

Yet it turns out that, if we were to help expose people who find maths tough to lots of numbers, lots of counting, and all sorts of number games from the very start of life—and if we make numbers real so we don't just have "two" but we have "two bananas" and we keep playing with numbers—maths can get better.

In fact, children benefit from having numbers in their lives from the start, all the time. For the dyscalculic child, this will gradually remove the mystery and horror of maths. For the child who is naturally bright at maths, he or she gets better and ever more enthusiastic about maths.

And in due course, that child will be asking such questions as: "What number did the Romans *not* have?" And with great pride, they will reveal: "It's zero. That very odd number. If you multiply or divide by zero, you get nothing. If you add or subtract zero, nothing changes!"

So, if you want your daughter or son or grandchild to be good at maths, talk numbers all the time. Play with numbers, use numbers, explore numbers, make numbers part of their daily lives.

In short, use this book. It really will be worth it.

Tony Attwood

C.Ed., B.A., M.Phil (Lond), F.Inst.A.M., founder,
The Dyscalculia Centre (https://dyscalculia.me.uk)

1

INTRODUCTION

"Encouraging parents to talk about numbers with their babies, and providing them with effective ways to do so, may positively impact children's school achievement."

– SUSAN LEVINE,
Professor, Department of Psychology,
University of Chicago

DAY 1

Your Newborn Baby Already Understands So Much

Mathematics is an essential skill to master, especially in our increasingly digital environment. Adults need to use maths skills every day, and yet poor numeracy remains endemic in the UK and worldwide. Government statistics suggest that 17 million adults in the UK have the numeracy level expected of primary school children.[1] How can we change this for the next generation? What is your role?

First, you need to believe that maths is an area of your baby's development worth investing your time in. With so many classes and activities available to your baby, how do you decide which ones are important?

Maybe understanding that your baby is *already* a budding maths genius will persuade you.

At just a few hours old, babies begin to categorise. They will use their amazing mathematical skills to first identify faces and then to subcategorise them into Mummy, Daddy or strangers. Do you need further evidence?

Fortunately, plenty exists. For example, professors Arlette Streri and Véronique Izard of Université de Paris found newborns were already able to associate the number of syllables heard with the number of shapes they were shown—and that's from within only seven to 100 hours of being born![2]

Their study involved playing either four or 12 syllables to each newborn, e.g. "tuuuuu-tuuuuu-tuuuuu-tuuuuu" or "tu-tu-tu-tu-tu-tu -tu-tu-tu-tu-tu-tu". While the syllables kept playing in the background, the baby was then shown images of either four or 12 shapes. The newborns consistently showed a preference for the image with the same number of shapes as the syllables played. What impressive numeracy skills at just a few hours old!

► ACTIVITY ◄

Help your baby with classification

Hold your baby in a loving, nurturing way and spend time bonding. Talk and smile. Help your baby feel confident and loved, which sets the stage for doing the hard maths work of classifying and understanding the world. Notice and reward your baby's ability to categorise you as someone who is trustworthy.

The simple experience of feeling loved helps develop your baby's brain. Pour on the love!

★ ★ ★ ★ ★ ★ ★

Don't underestimate your baby's ability to start exploring maths. With a seemingly innate number sense, now is the time!

DAY 2

The Power of NUMBER TALK

Now you have decided you would like to nurture your baby's seemingly innate maths skills, what is the best way? Some parents get put off by thinking they do not have a strong enough maths understanding to teach their babies. Yet evidence shows the solution is astoundingly simple.

A few years ago, Susan Levine, a professor in the Department of Psychology at the University of Chicago, led a piece of research titled 'What Counts in the Development of Young Children's Number Knowledge?'.[3] Professor Levine monitored children interacting at home with a parent and counted the quantity of number words used during normal play.

Her team recorded all uses of the numbers one to ten and found that the *quantity* of number words used in each family home varied hugely. Some parents used as few as four number words in 7½ hours of interaction; others used as many as 257 number words in that timeframe.

Previous studies indicated that children differ significantly from each other in their mathematical knowledge by the time they enter pre-school. Levine conducted her study to ascertain whether the differences in ability at the start of pre-school could be attributed to the exposure to number talk in the early years before school. There was a correlation. The more times parents used the number words "one" to "ten" during infancy, the better their children understood numbers when they were tested at four years old.

The message from this study is clear: to teach your baby maths, simply talk about numbers as often as possible. No need for expensive DVD sets or time-consuming flashcards; just count with your baby whenever you can.

As a guide, to align with parents who use the most "number talk" you would need to say at least 250 number words each day. If this sounds challenging, then remember: if you take your baby up and down the stairs five times a day and count the steps each time, you will probably have already clocked over 100 number words. But do not worry. This book provides plenty of additional ideas, activities, and tools to help you maintain high levels of number talk each day.

▶ A C T I V I T Y ◀

Count number words

Set aside a five-minute session and count how many number words you can use in that time. This could be counting the ducks at the park, numbers found in a bedtime story, or even saying out loud the number of buttons you do up as you dress your baby. It takes less than a minute to sing 'Five Little Speckled Frogs' and you will have said 16 number words in that time.

★ ★ ★ ★ ★ ★

Any parent can teach their baby maths—simply talk about numbers as often as you can.

DAY 3

Maths Ability is the Strongest Predictor of Later Academic Achievement

From the 'Talk, Read, Sing!' campaign to closing the 30-million-word gap, parents are becoming better informed about the importance of early literacy. Yet it is often presumed to be fine if children tackle maths later—or not even consider it before formal schooling commences. However, research shows that early exposure to maths can influence a child's later academic success.

Professor Greg Duncan led a study titled 'School readiness and later achievement'.[4] This study researched the links between key elements of school readiness and later school reading and maths achievement levels. The research concluded that the strongest predictors of later achievement were school-entry maths, reading, and attention skills. In fact, maths ability was by far the strongest predictor of academic achievement. Reading was half as strong, and attention less than a quarter as strong a predictor compared to maths.

Importantly, the study also found that pre-school maths skills such as knowing numbers are equally good predictors of future reading achievement. That means early development of mathematical skills can also lead to future reading success. However, while pre-school reading skills are a good predictor of future reading achievement, they were found to be less correlated with future maths achievement. By

9

following the guidance in this book, you'll find that teaching your baby maths will also boost his or her literacy skills. Therefore, you need not choose between teaching literacy or numeracy. Why compromise any area of your baby's development?

It has also been found that the association between school-entry skills and later achievement declines more quickly over time for reading than for maths outcomes. So, it seems early maths skills not only are a better predictor of future academic achievement, but they pay larger dividends over a longer time than early reading skills, attention, or socio-emotional behaviours.

In short, if you only focus on one area of your baby's development, then mathematics is the best place to start!

► ACTIVITY ◄

Sing 'This Little Piggy Went to Market'

Introducing maths to your baby can be as easy as singing 'This Little Piggy Went to Market' while touching your baby's toes one at a time. Doing this will introduce the key mathematical areas of sequences and patterns in a silly, enjoyable way as well as developing verbal and attention skills as a bonus.

★ ★ ★ ★ ★ ★ ★

If you're not sure where to focus activity time with your baby, know this: Having strong maths ability at the time of school entry more strongly predicts later academic achievement than literacy skills.

2

NUMBER TALK

"The study of mathematics, like the Nile, begins in minuteness but ends in magnificence."

– CHARLES CALEB COLTON,
English cleric educated at Eton, 1804

DAY 4

NUMBER TALK Introduction

NUMBER TALK is the central theme of this book. You have already seen on DAY 2 that simply increasing the *quantity* of number words you say to your baby may increase his or her school-entry maths ability. Talk about maths as much as possible and increase the number of maths words you use each day. That sounds simple, but it is useful to consider a few tips that will make the most of this powerful activity.

During the next few days, follow the structure of a useful mnemonic based on the words NUMBER TALK. This will keep you on track and make sure you are never short of ideas on how to keep the NUMBER TALK flowing.

Name what you see   **T**ake turns
Undivided attention   **A**ctions
Maths   **L**a la la
Books   **K**eep praising
Enjoy!
Repetition

Your child will need to learn, understand, and apply more than 500 maths words in the first year of formal schooling. These contain everything from number and shape names to days of the week and prepositions. (Yes, you read that right, prepositions—in, on, off, down, up, etc—are key maths vocabulary. They fall under geometry, which is a branch of mathematics that studies the sizes, shapes, and positions of items.) Clearly, the more familiar your baby is with these words before entering school, the easier it will be to apply them and master the underlying maths concepts. However, do not be overwhelmed at the task of teaching your baby the language of maths. Among the most often used 100 general words are several mathematical words; in the top ten is the geometry positional word "in". Also featured in everyday vocabulary are these common words: "on", "one", "two", "day", "most", "time", "up", "first" and "over" (to name just a few).

Bear in mind that key mathematical words are already among the most often used words. By simply increasing the amount you talk to your baby, you will automatically be teaching maths basics.

► A C T I V I T Y ◄

Introduce the most often used
maths word—"in"

Focus today on noticing when you use the word "in" with your baby. Emphasise it and add actions to help your baby better understand this useful mathematical word. Using a silly, action-packed song like 'The Hokey Cokey' can make teaching your baby maths even more fun!

★ ★ ★ ★ ★ ★ ★

**Use the NUMBER TALK mnemonic to
increase the quantity of maths words you
say to your baby.
Teaching your baby maths can be that easy!**

DAY 5

NUMBER TALK: Name What You See

What simple advice will help you easily increase your word count when talking with your baby? Name what you see. Or, even better, name what your baby is looking at, pointing at, or touching.

Research shows that while talking to your baby is beneficial, you need to engage *directly* with him or her. Having background noise such as adult conversations, radio, or TV just won't cut it. If you talk directly about things in your baby's sightline, then you are likely to keep the interaction between you and your baby far more engaging for both of you. The words you say will have meaning and can help strengthen your baby's understanding.

By talking about actual things (e.g., "Let's have a big bowl of yummy pasta"), you can prompt yourself to use rich vocabulary involving all five senses. Your baby may have already noticed the smell of the cooking pasta. Having a name for your little one to link to the smell will help him or her connect with the sensations, which in turn will make the words memorable.

Once you get used to making a running commentary, it is not a huge leap to include mathematically focused words as you elaborate. Simple examples are:

"I'll put your shoes on" could become "I'll put your **two** shoes **on**, **left** foot **first**, then **right** foot **second**."

"Milk time!" could become "Here is a **big full** bottle of milk.

Wow, you already drank **half** of it! Now the bottle is **empty**!"

Naming what you see gives structure and purpose to your chat. As your general talking and verbal interactions increase, NUMBER TALK happens.

►ACTIVITY◄

Play two versions of 'Name What You See'

1. Talk out loud as you go about your chores to increase your general dialogue.
2. Give your baby focused time as you see what he or she is gazing at and explain what it is.

Either version of this game will benefit your baby and ally any worry about using number words. The more you talk, the more you will be able to introduce your baby to the language of maths.

* * * * * * *

Naming what you see gives structure and purpose to your chat. As your talking and verbal interactions increase, NUMBER TALK happens.

DAY 6

NUMBER TALK: Undivided Attention

Take a minute to picture these two mealtime scenarios:

Scenario one: "Here you are. You have one, two, three—there are three peas left. Delicious!"

Scenario two: "Oh yummy, you have one…" *Beep beep* (pause to check your text message). "Let's see, oh, I think you've eaten a pea, you've got two, that's one…" *Bing* (pause to reply to an email). "You've eaten all three peas, well done!"

The first scenario is clearly preferable when it comes to teaching the concept of counting, yet the second scenario is increasingly common. Parents may be *physically* spending more time with their babies but *mentally* are more and more distracted.

Putting maths to one side for a minute, let's consider what else is happening. Dr Tallie Z Baram, Professor of Paediatrics and Anatomy-Neurobiology at University of California, Irvine, and her colleagues, used a rat model to study how good, but disrupted, attention from mothers can affect their newborns.[5] To generate fragmented disrupted behaviours in mother rats, researchers put a reduced amount of bedding in one set of cages where a mother rat had a litter of newborn pups. The mother would look for additional bedding for nesting purposes, breaking up her care of the pups. As a result, she provided interrupted and unreliable attention to her pups.

These rats were compared to those in normal cage environments. When the offspring of these rats were fully grown, the research team compared their socialising and fun eating behaviours to that of their peers. They found that the baby rats with the disrupted attention demonstrated less pleasure and less of an ability to socialise.

It is unsettling to note that both sets of rats had normal weight, enough food, and were raised in the right temperature. What is more, they both spent the same amount of time with their mothers. The only difference was in the type of attention the rats received from their mothers. The mothers of the pups in the modified environment tended to be more fragmented and unpredictable than those in the proper environment.

While humans are clearly not rats, this study gives us food for thought. It highlights that, when communicating with your baby, you want to allocate special time that provides your baby with your undivided attention. This is not only about teaching maths; it is about raising an emotionally secure, well-adjusted child. All are worth investing in.

This undivided attention can start at any age. When giving your full focus to a newborn, holding your baby a distance of eight to 12 inches from your face is ideal. See if your baby is awake and alert before trying to engage. Observe his or her body language and facial expressions. Listen to the sounds being made. Look into your baby's eyes. Match your facial expression and tone of voice to your baby's response.

Let your baby lead the conversation and, if cooing, quietly match your tone to his or hers. If your baby looks away, now is not the time to initiate an interactive session. Simply rely on your baby to let you know when it's time for you to give your undivided attention.

►ACTIVITY◄

The sequences and patterns of coos

1. Turn off your phone.
2. Have a "must do today" list to ensure you are not constantly distracted by chores.
3. Do not go on autopilot when parenting. Be mindful and stay in the moment.

These simple steps will enable your baby to learn much from you. To give this time a focus on maths, simply imitate and repeat your baby's "coos" as a way to teach sequences and patterns. Exploring patterns now will help your baby spot them more easily in the future. Noticing patterns is important for many aspects of mathematics. For example, a prescriptive pattern of numbers—one, two, three, and so on—underpins the counting sequence.

These early introductions of maths concepts should be natural and relaxed rather than structured and intense.

★ ★ ★ ★ ★ ★ ★

The *quantity* of your interactions with
your baby are important.
The *quality* is crucial.

DAY 7

NUMBER TALK: Maths

The study by Professor Levine described on DAY 2 focused on using the numbers one to ten as much as possible to give your baby a head start in maths. But maths is much more than learning number names or how to count.

To make this huge topic manageable, it is worthwhile to cover all the core areas early—you might be surprised to discover how much your baby already understands! This will enable you to better understand what your baby can already do and how you can build on that knowledge. (Each key area of school-entrance-level maths including counting, addition, subtraction, measuring, time, and geometry will be addressed in section 5 of this book.)

Children might excel at counting and addition but stop feeling confident when they are expected to tackle fractions and probability. By introducing the vocabulary and principles of all areas of maths in infancy, you can help your baby avoid forming fears about unknown topics.

▶ ACTIVITY ◀

Notice the maths around you

Think about what you are doing or saying and notice which area of maths is involved. Here are a few examples:

Addition – When you ask your baby about one more tickle, you are using the maths language of addition.

Shape – When you pass a block so your baby can build a tower, you are introducing a cube shape.

Position – When you pick up your baby, you use the mathematical geometry position word "up".

Measurement – When you prepare your baby's bottle, you fill it to 100ml or half full.

Maths is everywhere when you consciously notice it!

Embrace all areas of maths as your baby's curiosity leads you to discuss addition, subtraction, geometry, and measurement. You'll discover there's more to maths than number names and counting!

DAY 8

NUMBER TALK: Books

Arguably one of the easiest ways to add NUMBER TALK to your daily routine is to invest in a few books or borrow some from your local library. Reading books to your baby is a fun way to pass the time. If those books also include numbers, shapes, patterns, or other areas of maths, then that will help build your baby's maths vocabulary and confidence.

Books are portable, easy to obtain, and universally loved by babies. While best known for improving literacy, they also bring a lot of maths benefits. Here are a few:

1. Regular sharing of stories has been shown to correlate with better self-control, increased attention span, and higher IQ compared with children who aren't read stories.
2. Books are colourful, interactive, and a fun way to introduce numbers, counting, shapes, and prepositions as well as any other maths topic you might choose.
3. Stories can be used to introduce causality, sequences, and logic in a relaxed, happy environment that your baby will look forward to each day.

What better way to teach your baby maths and introduce NUMBER TALK!

► ACTIVITY ◄

Read your baby 'The Very Hungry Caterpillar'

A book such as *The Very Hungry Caterpillar* by Eric Carle that teaches numbers and days of the week will certainly help your baby learn about maths. But you could choose any baby book. Most will include shapes in the pictures that you can point to or sets of items you can count for your baby. You can even add your own maths to reading a book by saying "I am going to start on the **first** page…"

★ ★ ★ ★ ★ ★ ★

Babies love books! Babies love learning!
Share a story today to boost your baby's maths
development and other skills, too.

DAY 9

NUMBER TALK: Enjoy!

You only need to spend a few minutes with babies to see how drawn they are to faces. At a few hours old, you may have noticed how your baby could differentiate your face from a stranger's face. This high-speed development continues, so that within a few days, your baby could distinguish between facial expressions and emotions such as happiness, sadness, fear, and surprise.

Soon, your baby learns to use information from other people's faces to work out what to do in new situations. For example, when your baby is first crawling and comes across a possibly dangerous slope, he or she might look to your facial expressions for cues and only attempt to descend the slope once you offer an encouraging smile.

Why is this important? If you dislike maths, then your baby will dislike it too. If you enjoy talking about maths—if you are animated, smiling, and having fun—your baby will learn it is a positive thing. Your facial expressions and body language will tell your baby if maths is a good thing or not.

Every time you teach your baby maths, make sure the experience is fun for both of you.

►ACTIVITY◄

Sing a silly song

Choose a song that makes you smile as you sing it. Something like 'Zoom Zoom Zoom We're Flying to the Moon' is a great way to introduce number words while counting down to the big lift off. Maths really can be fun!

★ ★ ★ ★ ★ ★ ★

Your baby trusts you.
If you enjoy maths, he or she will, too!

DAY 10

NUMBER TALK: Repetition

What are your baby's first words likely to be? In England, they tend to be "Mama" and "Dadda". However, in France it might be "Maman" and "Papa". Put simply, babies repeat the words they hear the most. It is up to *you* which words you want your baby to hear and learn.

Many factors go into a baby learning a new word. Most parents have direct experience of their child learning certain inappropriate words after hearing them only once! However, in general, repetition helps with learning and with clarifying meaning.

When repeating a word, it can be useful to consider the five senses. If you're teaching the word "dog", for instance, then just hearing the word in conversation will make it familiar. However, showing your baby a picture of a dog in a book while saying "Dog!" will be more interesting. Better yet, let your baby meet a real dog so he or she can hear the word while seeing, touching, and even smelling it. That will make the word "dog" particularly memorable.

Because the language of maths can be abstract, repetition highlights what certain maths words actually relate to. The much-quoted '10,000 hours to be a concert pianist' theory is likely over-generalised. However, its underlying principle of 'practice makes perfect' still applies, especially when learning new words.

►ACTIVITY◄

Teach your baby the number one

Today, teach your baby the number "one" using repetition. For example, replicate this conversation:

"You have **one** sock on!"

At this point, your baby is just becoming familiar with the sounds of the words, so to help with understanding, hold up one sock.

"Look! **One** sock."

After seeing the sock, your baby now focuses on the noun in the sentence.

Next, use the number "one" in repeated phrases.

"I'm going to put **one** sock on **one** foot."

This sentence highlights the different items (sock and foot) as you name them, with the similarity being the number of items (one).

Learning new words is tricky, but by using repetition, even the hardest words will become familiar to your baby soon enough.

The language of maths can be developed through repetition and confidence.
It's up to *you* which words you want your baby to hear and learn.

DAY 11

NUMBER TALK: Take Turns

Before addressing the how and why of taking turns with a baby who cannot yet talk, let's consider if it's even possible for a baby to take turns with someone else in a conversation.

A study titled 'Early development of turn-taking in vocal interaction between mothers and infants'[6] which was led by Professor Maya Gratier, confirmed evidence of babies as young as eight weeks demonstrating the skill of turn-taking. This study also showed that infants adjust the quality of their conversation in response to the quality and timing of adult conversations they hear.

Professor Gratier monitored the quality of turn-taking by recording the mums and their babies in their own homes. The mums were instructed to hold their babies facing them and then talk to them in their usual manner for ten minutes without the use of toys or singing. Afterwards, the data was used to record and analyse the vocalisations and pauses between each mum and baby. It was discovered that the turn-taking witnessed was in line with the frequency and duration identified between adults engaged in conversation. This indicates that babies are able to take turns from as young as eight weeks old.

Why is taking turns important? It's a crucial part of social interaction and an important introduction to maths through a repeating pattern. Given your baby already excels at turn-taking, it makes sense to continue nurturing this skill.

Another study titled 'Language Exposure Relates to Structural Neural Connectivity in Childhood'[7] which was led by MIT graduate Rachel Romeo identified that the back-and-forth within conversations is more critical to language development than the quantity of words spoken. This study counted the number of conversational turns and the response time between exchanges. The data was then compared to brain scans. The researchers found that greater conversational turn-taking was associated with stronger connections between two brain regions that are central to the comprehension and production of speech. Families' socioeconomic backgrounds did not appear to influence the results.

The key to turn-taking with your baby is being fully focused on him or her while talking or playing. Be responsive to all the cues, such as picking up your baby when crying. Simply responding to your baby's needs demonstrates to him or her the value of communicating. You can also introduce other turn-taking games such as rolling a ball back and forth, alternating who places the next block on a tower, or even playing peek-a-boo.

The earliest conversations with babies involve their bodies and their eyes. It can be easy to overlook the importance of responding to their actions, but remember, infants are hard-wired to understand turn-taking. Taking the time to acknowledge and respond to their actions will reinforce this essential skill.

▶ ACTIVITY ◀

Play peek-a-boo

Peek-a-boo is a classic game that has been played for generations—and for good reason.

In its simplest form, peek-a-boo is played by hiding your eyes behind your hands, then saying "peek-a-boo" as you open your hands and reveal your face. Your baby loves your face and your voice, and will revel in the visual, auditory, and social interaction this game creates.

Peek-a-boo is a straightforward, enjoyable method of introducing turn-taking. You take your turn when you cover your face and say, "Peek-a-boo" and your baby follows in turn, which might involve giggling, cooing, or (later), saying "more" or "again". Then when your baby looks at you, it signals that it's your turn to hide again. The repeated pattern of taking turns with your baby reinforces the important maths area of sequences. Who knew that teaching your baby maths could be so entertaining and easy!

Taking turns is an important part of social interaction and a valuable introduction to the patterns within maths.

DAY 12

NUMBER TALK: Actions

Actions speak louder than words. When it comes to communicating with your baby, this is certainly true. You might wait months to hear a first word spoken!

Research shows that babies can learn their first basic signs as young as six months old. Dr Joseph Garcia, author of *Sign with Your Baby*, noted that babies six to seven months old who are frequently and consistently shown sign-language signs can use them to communicate by eight or nine months. That indicates it's wise to introduce simple signs early. If you do, your baby will likely be able to sign even before he or she can talk!

Should you teach your baby sign language? Beyond the benefits of reinforcing the language of maths, your baby's levels of frustration can be lessened by reducing the gap between a baby's desire to communicate what's needed and an ability to do so. Some experts also assert that the use of signing can be linked to psychological benefits, including higher confidence and improved self-esteem.

As with so many other methods of teaching, introducing signs and actions not only increases your baby's cognitive ability and maths knowledge, it helps with all areas of development. Dr Gwyneth Doherty-Sneddon, a psychologist at the University of Stirling, reviewed multiple studies[8] on this topic and found that communication is at the heart of child development—be it cognitive, social, emotional, or behavioural.

Embrace this knowledge and know that teaching your baby maths by verbal or sign communication will bring all sorts of benefits.

►ACTIVITY◄

Teach your baby signing

Look for a local baby signing group, perhaps at your library or Sure Start Centre. Alternatively, research free online resources that show you the basic signs. You will probably start with simple gestures for "thirsty", "hungry" and "tired", but it's easy to include these maths signs, too:

- More: To do the sign for more, flatten out your hands and bring your thumbs under to make an O shape. Then bring your hands together and separate them repeatedly.
- Numbers: Hold up one finger to represent the number one, two fingers for two, etc.
- Circle: Hold out one index finger. Take the opposite index finger and make a circle starting and ending at the first index finger.

★ ★ ★ ★ ★ ★ ★

Actions make words come to life for babies. *Show* your baby maths to make the concepts real.

DAY 13

NUMBER TALK: La La La

Singing nursery rhymes is fun! They are great for introducing phonics, rhyming, and musical skills such as pitch and volume. But are they useful for improving maths ability? Absolutely!

To instantly increase your NUMBER TALK, go for a number song such as, 'One, Two, Three, Four, Five Once I Caught a Fish Alive', 'Hickory Dickory Dock', or 'Zoom, Zoom, Zoom We're Going to the Moon'.

The beauty of songs and rhymes is that they are memorable. Nursery rhymes consist of a simple, catchy melody with repeating phrases, making them ideal for both you and your baby to remember. They are so easy to repeat, you might find yourself still humming the tune hours later.

However, do not feel you are restricted to number songs to teach your baby maths. Other key maths areas are patterns and sequences, and nursery rhymes and songs nearly always follow a clear, simple sequence of events. Most rhymes have a beginning, middle, and end, and they introduce new ideas as they go. Rhymes such as 'Humpty Dumpty' or 'Mary had a Little Lamb' are good examples of stories within a song. While keeping your baby's attention and entertaining them, they are also teaching him or her about maths.

Nearly all nursery rhymes contain maths words. Think of any

rhyme. Even if it does not have numbers or counting, it will likely have shapes or sizes or prepositions such as "on" or "in". For example, by singing a well-known song such as 'Jack and Jill Went up the Hill' you are teaching your baby the maths concepts of "up" and "down".

Most importantly, singing to your baby is an engaging, enjoyable experience!

►ACTIVITY◄

Sing 'Tiny Tim'

Rhymes are often silly with their unexpected words or noises and funny actions your baby will love. To begin singing to your baby, start with nursery rhymes or songs you enjoy and are familiar to you. You can consider going to a rhyme time session, buying a book to learn new songs or even making up your own songs. Rhyme them if you can and add actions if you want to. Your baby will love the gentle sing-song sound of your voice.

A fun rhyme for today is 'Tiny Tim'. You can make this rhyme more interesting for your baby by using hand actions to act it out. Interlock your fingers to make your hands into Tim, the turtle. Sing it at bath time and emphasise the maths word "in" by dipping your hands into the bath water before Tiny Tim eats up all the soap. Use the build-up to the end "pop" to get your baby involved and excited!

★ ★ ★ ★ ★ ★ ★

Nursery rhymes are full of maths-rich vocabulary,
patterns, sequences, and fun.
They are like rocket fuel for your baby's
maths development!

DAY 14

NUMBER TALK: Keep Praising

Giving praise is important for so many reasons.

To begin with, babies are born with an innate desire to please. If they engage in NUMBER TALK and you praise them, they will have the motivation to do it again. It is as simple as that!

On a deeper level, the number of positive verbal interactions parents have with their babies correlates with the overall number of words spoken.

Fundamentally, whether you are a talkative or non-talkative parent, there is a minimum number of verbal interactions you will have each day. If your baby reaches out and touches a hot oven, for example, you will immediately shout "Stop!"

Consider when you are hosting a play date and your attention is on the other adults. You're making them drinks, discussing how little sleep you have had, and so on. Imagine your baby is cooing happily on the playmat. In this scene, it's unlikely you will invest time in communicating directly with your baby. Next, imagine your toddler is colouring quietly. Again, your full focus remains on the adults.

Now picture your baby grabbing at another baby on the playmat and that baby cries. You might immediately respond by moving your baby away and saying something like "No grabbing!" Or suppose your toddler snatches a pen from another toddler. That gets your attention, and you quickly jump in with "No snatching. You have to share."

These scenarios show that unless you make a conscious effort to use positive verbal communication, then the balance of interactions is likely to fall towards the negative.

It is fine to sometimes be distracted and only respond to your child when parental guidance is needed. But when you hear yourself using a sharp tone of voice, remind yourself of the importance of positive parental interactions and then say several positive things to your child. Some people suggest you should aim for as many as *ten* positive statements for every *one* negative comment. No doubt, the more the better. However, for now, aim for the more achievable target of *five* positive interactions for every negative comment.

For example, to your toddler who is drawing quietly, you might say:

1. "What a lovely picture you have drawn."
2. "The yellow pen was the perfect choice to make the sun look big and bright."
3. "You have been concentrating so well on this."
4. "I notice you've been sharing your other five pens very nicely."
5. "Well done for putting your drink up on the side so it doesn't spill over your colouring."

Comments like these may initially feel forced but using the Rule of Five Positives for every negative comment reminds you to keep praising your child. Take care to avoid only saying something when an issue needs to be addressed—on the one occasion when a drink spills rather than on the 20 other times it has been carefully kept out of the way. Again, remember the Rule of Five Positives.

Praise is also absolutely appropriate for NUMBER TALK. Not only does it increase the flow of conversation and the number of interactions, it also guides your baby to better understand what is important to you. If your baby shows an interest in numbers, don't let these moments slide past unnoticed. Make sure to encourage it by using praise. Your baby will be more interested in maths in the future if his or her infancy is filled with positive touchpoints related to numbers.

► ACTIVITY ◄

Use the Rule of Five Positives

Incorporate the Rule of Five Positives today by making eye contact and smiling while saying a positive word like "Wow!" or "Yes!" Start your positive interactions when your baby coos or points. For example, say "Yes! That is a **big** bubble!" (To highlight the maths areas of size and shape) or "Wow! Your bowl is **empty**!" (To highlight the maths area of measurement). These positive interactions give you a chance to highlight maths concepts in an encouraging way and keep the maths vocabulary flowing.

★ ★ ★ ★ ★ ★ ★

Your baby was born with an innate desire to please. If your little one engages with NUMBER TALK and you give praise, he or she will engage even more. It's as simple as that!

DAY 15

NUMBER TALK Summary

You now have a clear idea of how to fit as much NUMBER TALK into your baby's day as possible. It's hard to believe babies can comprehend the meaning of many words before they can talk or even point. However, researchers have shown how advanced their receptive language—their understanding of the spoken word—actually is.

Dr Elika Bergelson led and published a study in 2012 titled 'At 6–9 months, human infants know the meanings of many common nouns'.[9] She found that babies aged six to nine months could demonstrate their understanding of spoken words by directing their gaze to the pictures that were named. Until then, it was commonly believed this level of comprehension of language did not develop until closer to 12 months.

For example, as part of an experiment, the babies were shown pairs of images, one food related and one a body part. The babies then heard a statement such as, "Where's the apple?" to see if their eyes would move to the relevant object on the screen. Researchers found the babies fixed their gaze more often on the picture that was being named than the other image.

The conclusion? When you talk to babies, they will understand more than you expect. *You* can choose what language to introduce your baby to on a repeated basis, including certain key words daily. The more they hear, the more they learn.

Hopefully, knowing how clever your baby already is motivates you to use these NUMBER TALK suggestions and talk about maths as much as possible with your baby. Here is a review:

Name what you see – Make it real, make it visual, and emphasise the maths words.

Undivided attention – Turn off your phone and make eye contact with your baby.

Maths – Don't just talk about numbers; include all areas of mathematics.

Books – Use books to make learning new maths words interesting.

Enjoy! – Have fun with the activities and encourage your baby to love maths.

Repetition – The more often they hear maths vocabulary, the better.

Take turns – Give your baby time to "coo" and "gurgle" while you "chat".

Actions – Lift your baby high when saying "up".

La la la – Sing nursery rhymes and number songs that are catchy and fun.

Keep praising – Let your baby know you are proud.

► ACTIVITY ◄

Have a conversation with your baby

Now is the perfect time to have a conversation. Repeat your baby's noises, make eye contact, and nod as he or she gurgles and coos at you. You can simply respond with an enthusiastic "Yes, I agree!" or "You're so right!"

The more parents positively engage with babies, the more they will use their voices and listen. By focusing on NUMBER TALK, you will not only help breech the 30-million-word gap but many of those words will have a numeracy focus.

The more talkative you are, the more your baby will naturally learn the language of maths.

★ ★ ★ ★ ★ ★ ★

Your baby already understands so
much of what you say.
The more you use NUMBER TALK, the more
maths your baby will absorb.

COUNTING

"An obvious manifestation of counting happens as children learn to speak and use sounds that refer to quantity. Delighted adults begin to use rhymes, stories, and songs to teach them the number names, and are soon rewarded by children repeating them. Proud parents relate that they can count to three, later, ten and so on.

"There is however much more to counting than repeating sounds. It entails doing many things at once like rubbing your tummy and patting your head, only more complicated and with a purpose you need to be aware of."

– LES STAVES,
author, *Mathematics for Children with Severe and Profound Learning Difficulties*

DAY 16

Counting Overview

NUMBER TALK is important. If you are saying numbers to your baby a lot, the next natural step is to teach him or her how to count. Sounds simple enough, right?

If you ask parents if their toddlers are showing early signs of maths ability, they may proudly announce they can already count to three. This is fantastic. They are right to be proud. But there is more to counting than remembering the numbers one, two, three.

Introducing numbers in sequence, or rote counting, tends to be an area of mathematics that parents feel comfortable with. But are you, like many parents, inadvertently confusing your baby?

Professor Kevin Durkin[10] and his team studied language used by mothers and their children aged nine to 36 months. He found that numbers were commonly used in phrases such as "one, two, three, go" or "one, two, three, tickly," rather than the mathematically correct "one, two, three, four."

Mothers also asked children to repeat the number they had just said, resulting in jointly constructed number strings such as "one, one, two, two, three, three." The study focused on the many uses of number words and the inconsistencies in parental input, which can lead to short-term mismatches in their understanding of counting. It concluded that the way parents use numbers may be challenging and often ambiguous to infants.

Any number talk is good, but what might feel like a simple demonstration turns out to be complex for infants to decode. Remarkably, they do decode them! Keep counting in any form, and they will keep learning.

So, do not be put off. It is fantastic to use numbers in any way and as often as possible. For example, nursery rhymes do not always count in a logical order but are still great for introducing your baby to numbers. Babies need to get comfortable with number names and hear them often before they will truly grasp the concept of counting. However, by taking time to understand the full process of counting, you can help your baby when starting to talk to move from rote counting to fully appreciating the point of counting. The point is, in fact, to understand how many items are included in a set.

The more *you* understand the complexities of counting, the easier you can make it for your baby to master. The Five-Step Counting Process covered in the next five days builds your knowledge. And knowledge is power!

►ACTIVITY◄

Make a number mobile

Make a simple mobile to hang above your baby's cot, changing table, or bouncy chair. If your baby is less than six weeks old, then black and white items will catch his or her attention; after that, bright colours will be more engaging.

To make your mobile, attach two sticks in a cross shape and hang items from these using strings. Then talk to your baby about the objects in view. Say things such as "Yes, that is **one** black **sphere** and **one** white **sphere**." As you add items, be sure to count them out loud: "There are **one**, **two** black **spheres** and **one**, **two** white **spheres**." Change the items regularly to keep your baby interested and to keep the NUMBER TALK flowing.

★ ★ ★ ★ ★ ★ ★

The more you understand the complexities of counting, the easier you can make it for your baby to master.
Don't be put off—use numbers in a variety of ways as often as possible.

DAY 17

The Five-Step Counting Process

Step 1: Each Item is Only Counted Once

In 1978, researchers Professor Rochel Gelman and Professor Randy Gallistel introduced the five principles of counting to help understand the complexity involved in counting a simple group of items. For the next few days, we will consider one principle at a time of this intricate process.

The first step reminds us that each item should only be counted once. If this seems obvious, ask toddlers to count the ducks in the pond. They will probably keep pointing and listing numbers until they reach the highest number they know.

To introduce this concept to babies, move the items to one side as you count them. For example, if they have three blueberries on a plate, say the number one as you pick up the first blueberry and move it away from the remaining two, then do the same for the other two blueberries. This teaches them to only count each item once and then move on to the next.

►ACTIVITY◄

Count sets of items

Find opportunities to count sets of items when your baby is alert and engaged. For example, during tummy time on the playmat, you can move toys from one side of the mat to the other while counting them, showing you count each item once while teaching your baby the number words.

★ ★ ★ ★ ★ ★ ★

When counting a set of items, each item
is only counted once.
Show your baby this often by moving the items
to one side once they have been counted.

DAY 18

The Five-Step Counting Process

Step 2: Use the Numbers Learned in the Same Order Each Time

This is where rote counting—learning the sequence in which numbers are used—becomes important. Teaching your baby to use numbers in the *same* order each time is probably the easiest counting step to introduce. In all sorts of circumstances, you will find yourself listing the numbers in order, even when you are not actually counting a set of items.

You can reinforce this skill by singing lots of number nursery rhymes, reading number stories, and counting with your baby as often as possible. Repetition is key.

► ACTIVITY ◄

Sing 'One, Two, Three, Four, Five, Once I Caught a Fish Alive'

Sing a counting song like 'One, Two, Three, Four, Five, Once I Caught a Fish Alive' with your baby. The more interactive you can make it, the better. As you sing the numbers, hold up one finger, then two, and so on. If you have a toy fish or pictures of fish, point to them as you sing the numbers one, two, three, and so on—anything to make it more visual and entertaining for your baby.

★ ★ ★ ★ ★ ★ ★

When counting, use the numbers learned in the same order each time.
Repeat the sequence of numbers—one, two, three, and so on—as often as possible.

DAY 19

The Five-Step Counting Process

Step 3: The Final Number Represents
the Size of the Group of Items

Why do you count? To quantify a group of items. You already know
to count each item only once and to use the numbers in a set order.
However, to know there are three ducks in the pond, realise that the
most important number is the last number. This may sound obvious,
but because everything is new to your baby, it is a good time to make
this principle clear to him or her.

How? By repeating the last number like this: "Look, one, two,
three. There are three ducks in the pond today."

►ACTIVITY◄

Count your baby's fingers and toes

Find time to count your baby's fingers and toes today and emphasise the final number.

"Let me see…one, two, three, four, five, six, seven, eight, nine, ten toes. You have **ten** perfect toes!" Touch each toe as you count it and repeat as frequently as your baby finds it fun.

Reinforce this by reading the book *Ten Little Fingers and Ten Little Toes* by Mem Fox. The gentle rhyming nature of the prose—plus a lovely surprise kiss on the nose to end it—will make this a book your baby will love to hear many times.

★ ★ ★ ★ ★ ★ ★

Show your baby that the purpose of counting is to quantify a group of items. To indicate the total number of items, emphasise that the last number is the important one.

DAY 20

The Five-Step Counting Process

Step 4: Use Counting for Any Set— Real Objects or Imaginary Lists

Hopefully, you have spent the last few weeks talking to your baby constantly about numbers. But is all number talk equal?

Having discovered that the quantity of number talk used by parents directly affects a child's mathematical development, Professor Elizabeth Gunderson and Professor Susan Levine investigated whether some types of number talk are better than others in promoting mathematical understanding.[11]

Previous studies have shown that children who can count to ten may still not understand how to apply that skill to counting a specific set of objects. This step takes children from memorising numbers and rote counting to understanding numbers and applying their knowledge to real situations—an important development indeed.

During their research, Gunderson and Levine found some children can count a set of objects by the time they are three years old, but even by the age of four, others cannot. This led them to discover that, by the time children are four years old, there is already a one-to two-year gap in maths knowledge.

Early individual differences in children's mathematical knowledge would not be a problem if their schooling could easily overcome it. However, this does not often happen. If anything, the gap widens.

The study went on to discover that when parents used number words in a physical context—that is, to count a set of items that were present and visible to the infant—this proved more predictive of mathematical development than general number talk.

Intuitively, this makes sense. Having the set of objects visible makes an abstract concept, such as counting, more concrete and easier to understand. The presence of visible examples is particularly important given the difficulty of understanding number words. For example, the number word "eight" sounds identical to "ate" and "two" sounds the same as "too" and "to".

This might make you think you should stick to only counting visible items. But still, all number talk is beneficial. Your baby can manage more difficult concepts as long as you also keep reinforcing the basics.

Step 4 of the counting process highlights that, while children find it easier to count present, visible objects, introducing your baby to the idea that *anything* can be counted remains important. To support this, you would count things like hand claps or the number of "sleeps" until Granny visits.

It is also helpful to introduce mixed sets. For example, instead of only counting how many teddies your baby has, also count the number of toys of any type. This demonstrates that anything can be counted.

► ACTIVITY ◄

Play hide and seek

Given most infants do not walk until they are one or older, traditional hide and seek doesn't work with them. However, a lot of giggles (and a fair amount of maths learning) can be had by simply hiding your face behind your hands, a muslin, or a cushion while counting. To start, count to three then five and then ten or more. Finish with a big reveal—a "Boo!" or a tickle—to keep your baby engaged.

This introduction to hide and seek can develop into hiding behind a nearby chair and, when your baby is crawling, watching him or her attempt to find you.

Each time you play this game, you are teaching your baby the order of numbers in a fun way. This form of counting does not involve a real, visible set because it counts the passing of time. While this concept may be hard for your baby to grasp, it is still important to introduce it. The exciting nature of hide and seek keeps your baby wanting to play more, even though the counting is tricky.

★ ★ ★ ★ ★ ★ ★

Anything can be counted. Real objects are easier for your baby to understand, but imaginary lists—such as the passing of time— can also be introduced in a playful way.

DAY 21

The Five-Step Counting Process

Step 5: The Order of Counting Items Isn't Relevant

As previously established, the aim of counting a set of items is to find the total number. The order in which you count the items is not relevant; the total size of the group will always be the same.

It is a good idea to make this into a game. Count the set of items as normal the first time. On the second time of counting, to keep your baby interested, ask before you start, "I wonder how many there will be if I start from the other side of the group?" As you finish counting, pause for effect, then look surprised and state, "Wow, there were four again! Let's count them again, just to make sure…"

It is worth adding that it is not a good idea to count moving objects, such as children at the park or ducks in the pond, when introducing your baby to this particular counting principle!

►ACTIVITY◄

Count the same set of objects a few times, each time in a different order

If there are three cars in a line, then start from the left and count "One, two, three. There are three cars." Then start from the right and say "Let's just double check, one, two, three. There are three cars here." Finally, start in the middle and repeat the same sentence.

This shows your baby that the order of counting items does not affect the total number of objects.

★ ★ ★ ★ ★ ★

The order in which you count objects does not change the size of the group.

You can demonstrate this by counting the same group of items several times. Do it with a smile and a look of surprise when the total number *never* changes!

DAY 22

The Importance of Bigger Numbers

As you have seen over the last five days, counting is not quite as simple as it may first seem. Nor is talking about numbers. Finding that the quantity of number talk parents had with their child measurably affects later number knowledge, Professor Elizabeth Gunderson and Professor Susan Levine investigated this further.[11]

As noted on DAY 20, their research first highlighted that using numbers with visible sets was beneficial and helped babies learn numbers more effectively. However, they also discovered that using bigger numbers (this research looked specifically at numbers four to ten) was associated with better learning outcomes than using numbers one to three.

It seems there could be a link between the fact that, for sets of three or fewer objects, children don't always need to count the items to know the total. Infants are good at estimating or recognising the number of items without needing to count them. However, as the number of objects increases, a greater understanding of how numbers work is required.

This highlights the fact that you should never underestimate your baby. Do not think that teaching the numbers one to three is plenty. Babies are ready to absorb more information and learn far more complex things than you probably thought. Far from being a "pushy parent" if you introduce your baby to maths, your baby is ready to learn. Do not let it be *you* who holds back their natural desire to embrace maths.

▶ A C T I V I T Y ◀

Play tidy-up

Playing tidy-up with your baby can be a great way to teach them maths. Sort your baby's toys into sets: dolls, cars, blocks—whatever you have. For each pile, carefully count the number of toys it contains so your baby can see and hear what you are doing. Then count again as you put them in the box, thereby reinforcing the total number. Ideally, the number of items in each set should be larger than three, so mix up the sets if necessary.

★ ★ ★ ★ ★ ★ ★

**Counting with your baby as
often as possible is good.
Counting big sets of items is even better.**

4

DIFFICULTY OF MATHS

"If people do not believe that mathematics is simple, it is only because they do not realize how complicated life is."

– JOHN VON NEUMANN,
mathematician and author

DAY 23

Why is Maths So Hard?

This book is focused on helping your baby begin his or her formal maths education with confidence and interest. But why would it be necessary to invest this time? Is maths harder than other subjects?

To learn what people are thinking, start typing in an online search and see what it predicts, thereby showing you the most-asked questions. When you type "Why is maths…" the top responses include "so hard" and "so boring". Interestingly, if instead you type in "Why is reading…" the top five searches all include the word "important" with no mention of "hard" or "boring".

What does this tell us? Is maths actually hard? Or do we just perceive it as hard? One thing all parents know is that, with the world's ever-increasing dependency on technology, maths is definitely *important*, regardless of how hard or boring it may seem.

As a parent who wants your child to succeed, the next step is to work out what makes maths difficult. Follow that with determining how you can give your son or daughter the opportunity to not only achieve in maths but also enjoy the journey.

So why is maths so hard? In this section, you will look at a few issues people have with maths and get the information you need to ensure this need not be a problem for your baby.

►ACTIVITY◄

Play food fractions

Fractions are often considered a particularly hard part of maths in school. While giving your baby a snack, break it into two or four pieces and offer, for example, "half" a rice cake or a "quarter" of a banana. These words and concepts are as easy for your baby to learn as any other if they are talked about often enough.

At this age, you are your baby's primary influence. He or she looks to you to understand what is hard, scary, fun, or exciting. As your child enters school, peers and teachers will exert a greater influence than you. But for now, show that you think food fractions are fun, useful, and easy. Your baby will believe you!

★ ★ ★ ★ ★ ★ ★

Is maths hard? Is maths boring?
With your help, these opinions needn't
be true for your baby.
One thing is certain: Maths is important.

DAY 24

The Difficult Language

You will have noticed this book gives a lot of attention to frequently using the language of maths with your baby. The maths-related language expected from five-year-olds in school includes over 500 words. Parents confidently start teaching their toddlers the numbers one, two, three, and so on, but how many use the words "sphere" or "symmetrical" regularly? They also face the issue of different words meaning the same things—for example, two times two, two multiplied by two, double two, two lots of two—and the list goes on.

People invest a lot of time when learning languages such as French, Spanish, or German. But for maths, the focus is on learning the underlying concepts rather than the language used. Thus, not being familiar with the terminology can unnecessarily make simple exercises seem hard.

Let's take "probabilities" as an example of a tricky area of maths. A lot of school children groan at the thought of them. So, surely it is best to steer clear of this tricky concept when teaching your baby maths. Do you agree? You do not want your baby to think maths is too hard because of concepts such as this.

How would you even teach babies something as complex as probability? It turns out no teaching is required. Like so many areas of maths, they intuitively have a basic understanding of it, as the following study shows.

Research from Professor Fei Xu's Infant Cognition and Language

Lab in the Department of Psychology at UC Berkeley[12] showed that the average six-month-old is pretty good at understanding probabilities. In this study, babies were offered either a black or a pink lollipop. Whichever one they reached for was assumed to be their preferred colour. Once their preferences had been set, the babies were shown two pots of lollipops. One pot contained more pink lollipops and the other held more black ones. The researcher took a lollipop from each container, but only the stick was visible so the colour of the lollipop could not be seen. The babies were then allowed to select a lollipop. Amazingly, most of the time, they selected one from the pot that had more of their favourite colour. Without any teaching, they calculated that the probability of getting their desired lollipop would be higher when the pot has more lollipops of that colour.

This demonstrates how intelligent babies naturally are. And it prompts this question: If the underlying maths concepts are not difficult to understand, then how can you stop areas of maths from being perceived as "hard"?

You can maximise babies' potential by using the words they will need in later life to explain the mathematical concepts they remarkably know already.

Probabilities are not hard for babies. Do not let them think they are difficult when it's time to learn them at school. Investing time to build their confidence in the first year of their lives will be worthwhile for years to come.

► A C T I V I T Y ◄

Introduce probability vocabulary

To help you embrace the complexity of maths, use these "tricky" words and concepts of probability: "You like the blue ball best. You have **three** red balls and only **one** blue ball. So, the **probability** of your getting the blue ball is **low** compared with getting a red ball."

Embed this principle by turning the understanding of probability into an exciting game. Babies love the element of surprise such as toys with a character popping out of a barrel when sticks are inserted. But you don't know which stick will trigger it. Babies are too young to "slot" sticks, but they will likely be mesmerised by the process as they watch you. As you do it, say things like, "Look, there are **four** holes. If I put this **first** stick **in**, there is a **25 percent chance** the pirate will pop **out** of the barrel." Be sure to use words such as "likely, unlikely, likelihood, certain, uncertain, probable, possible, impossible, chance, risk, doubt".

In this way, you are teaching your baby the language of maths as early as possible.

★ ★ ★ ★ ★ ★ ★

Don't let the language of maths become a
barrier to your baby enjoying it.
Teach your little one the maths vocabulary
now before it feels "hard".

DAY 25

The Prevalence of Maths Anxiety

Breaking the maths anxiety cycle is tricky. Parents have been shown to influence their children's perception of maths by avoiding talking about it or even mentioning the subject in a negative way.

Personal fear of failure seems to be more prevalent in mathematics than any other subject, thereby further increasing children's maths anxiety.

The fact that maths questions are so often either right or wrong makes it hard to disguise failure. In subjects such as art or dance, self-belief can be nurtured even when the result may not be perfect. This is not always the case with mathematics. By helping your baby enjoy shapes, numbers, geometry, etc. as young as possible, you will instil a love of maths long before there is pressure from school tests.

Infants are born with a desire to understand the world around them, a love of learning, and a determination to discover more. By showing your baby you value maths and enjoy it, you have taken away one of the biggest barriers to being good at maths.

▶ A C T I V I T Y ◀

The power of positive affirmations

Your baby was born with no maths anxiety; make sure you are not the one to change that! How? By using positive affirmations.

In essence, a positive affirmation is a statement used to challenge negative thoughts or reinforce positive ones. In the same way your baby's neurological pathways are strengthened by repeating actions or hearing words repeated, MRI evidence suggests certain neural pathways are increased when people practise self-affirmation tasks.

Use the following positive affirmations today or make up your own:

"Let's see if we can spot any numbers on our walk today. **I love numbers!**"

"Shall we count the pieces of broccoli so we can share them equally? **Maths is so useful!**"

"Would you like to look at the shapes book? **I love to learn more maths every day!**"

★ ★ ★ ★ ★ ★ ★

Babies are not born with maths anxiety.
Rather, they're born with open, curious
minds and a desire to learn.

DAY 26

Is Maths Relevant?

The subject matter taught every day in hundreds of classrooms across the country does not always readily translate to real life. Maths can appear to be abstract and not entirely relevant beyond the need to pass exams. For example, how many people use trigonometry daily?

It is hard for children to stay interested in a subject just for the sake of passing an exam. And once you lose their interest, the subject becomes a chore. They might then find it hard, boring, or both.

The solution is simple. *Make maths come to life for them.* Start right now when they are babies enthralled by everything you show them. There are so many opportunities to wow them with the fascinating world of maths. You can help the concepts they will learn at school be relevant and real to them.

►ACTIVITY◄

The Golden Ratio

Take an abstract concept such as the Golden Ratio, also called the Fibonacci Sequence. The pattern starts like this: 0,1,1, 2, 3, 5, 8, 13, 21, in which two numbers are added together to make the next number. What's amazing is that if you look at the centre of a sunflower, each ring of seeds correlates to this Fibonacci Sequence. Show your baby this, count the seeds, and use the technical mathematical terms. Children may or may not remember this when taught about it in the classroom, but they will remember enjoying learning about maths.

If parents bring maths to life throughout their children's lives, those lucky children will understand that even the most dry, abstract principles taught in class have intriguing real-life applications.

★ ★ ★ ★ ★ ★

Make maths relevant by bringing it
to life for your baby.
Maths is everywhere, and your baby will
love exploring it every day with you.

DAY 27

Unknown End Goal

During their formative years, babies and toddlers will have stories read to them and will see adults reading books. That gives them an idea of what the goal is with literacy and reading. They work from picture board books onwards with an understanding of the format and structure of books. Ultimately, almost all learn to read fluently and achieve that goal.

When it comes to maths, it is much less common for young children to have a parental role model to emulate in the home environment. If a child does not understand the goal, then it can be hard to stay motivated.

Maths is the type of subject you can keep learning forever. For some, this is a joy; for others, it can seem like a never-ending task that gets harder and harder.

As a parent, when your children enter school, you can familiarise yourself with the curriculum and help them by introducing relevant topics into your general conversation. Show them how topics link. Explain what is likely to be covered next. Prepare them for new ideas and, where necessary, recap old areas. Most of all, if you can fill them with a love of maths, then they can enjoy each new topic without needing an end goal in mind!

For now, your baby won't be worried about an end goal, so feel free to set your own achievable goals such as introducing key maths vocabulary. As far as your baby is concerned, it's about just having fun with maths today.

►ACTIVITY◄

Blow raspberries on your baby's tummy

Teaching your baby maths can be as fun and simple as blowing raspberries! Either count forward as you're about to do a tummy raspberry—"one, two, three…"—or count backward to build the suspense—"five, four, three, two, one"—or count the raspberries as you deliver them.

Who cares about end goals when the process of learning can be so fun!

★ ★ ★ ★ ★ ★ ★

Forget about any "end goal" of
teaching your baby maths.
Let your baby lead the way and have fun
exploring the maths you come across together.

DAY 28

Building Blocks

The latter parts of the maths syllabus build on the early years of learning. With other subjects, your children might cover a specific period in history or a style of art. If they struggle with one aspect of it, you know not to worry; they will move on to a new topic in a couple of weeks. With maths, though, it is essential that your child fully masters each level before moving on. It is impossible to learn addition if he or she cannot count!

Unfortunately, the pace at which schools must teach mathematics can put some pupils at a disadvantage. Parents are best positioned to fill any knowledge gaps in a relaxed home environment. Your goal is to make maths accessible and manageable. That's why, starting well before their school days, gives them strong building blocks.

As you communicate, make maths real. For example, counting finger foods by touching and eating them is more memorable than being told, "One, two, three is how you count".

In the next section, you will read about the many areas of maths you can reinforce with your baby to provide the most robust start to his or her formal maths education.

►ACTIVITY◄

Enjoy a number walk

A basic foundation to all future maths is learning the numbers. This includes understanding that numbers represent quantities, have names, and work in sequences. It also includes knowing the symbol for each number; for example, number one is written as 1 and number twenty-three is written as 23.

To reinforce this concept and put building blocks in place for future written mathematics, take your baby on a number walk. You will find numbers everywhere—on signs, on doors, written on the pavement.

Start looking for the number one as you walk. Then, as you spot it as the symbol 1, point it out to your baby. When you have spotted a few number ones, then move on to number two and look for it written as 2.

You might be surprised how quickly your baby picks up on this idea heading towards his or her first year. And toddlers may well continue the fun and lead the number walk.

★ ★ ★ ★ ★ ★ ★

**Start now to build firm foundations for
your baby's maths journey.
Use NUMBER TALK to guide you.**

DAY 29

Dyscalculia or Maths Dyslexia

One condition that can genuinely result in maths being hard for you or your baby is dyscalculia, sometimes referred to as maths dyslexia. DSM-5 defines dyscalculia as "a specific learning disorder, an impediment in mathematics, evidencing problems with number sense, memorisation of arithmetic facts, accurate and fluent calculation, and accurate math reasoning".

You will not know for a few years if your baby is one of the two to six percent of individuals who fall into this category. However, tools used to help children learn mathematics when they are dyscalculic are just as relevant to teaching your baby maths. They include:

- make maths real and visible.
- take an active interest to role model that maths can be fun.
- continually build your baby's self-esteem and stay motivated.
- be especially vigilant about maths anxiety, which can exacerbate existing processing issues.

In essence, if your baby ends up finding maths hard because of dyscalculia, it becomes even more valuable to set in motion the best start possible. It's a good investment.

►ACTIVITY◄

Roll the dice

Buy a large foam dice or make your own using cardboard with drawn-on dots. Ronit Bird, a specialist in dyscalculia and arithmetic difficulties, asserts the importance of recognising number *patterns* instead of counting individual dots each time. Knowing the number without counting—subitising—is something babies are naturally good at, but it can be delayed in those with dyscalculia.

To make this learning activity fun, roll the dice while letting your baby look at the pattern of dots on them. Say the number out loud, then add an action to it. For example, if you roll a three, then say, "I rolled a three, so you get three bounces! One! Two! Three!" You could easily do three tickles or three tummy raspberries instead of bounces.

Make maths real and visible, role model that it's fun, build your baby's self-esteem and be vigilant for maths anxiety.
Good advice for every parent.

5

AREAS OF
MATHEMATICS

"Mathematics is the science of patterns, and nature exploits just about every pattern that there is."

- IAN STEWART,
Professor of Mathematics,
University of Warwick

DAY 30

Areas of Mathematics Overview

So far, this book has looked at the importance of using numbers with your baby and the best way to teach him or her to count. However, the subject of mathematics, even when only considering the Early Years Curriculum, is broader than numbers and counting.

The first Mathematics National Curriculum, which starts at Key Stage 1, can be split into the following three areas:

1. Number – includes number and place value, comparing and ordering, addition and subtraction
2. Measurement – includes time and sequences
3. Geometry – includes properties of shapes, position and direction

In a pre-school setting, when children are observed during free play, these three categories of maths play are already consistently apparent:

1. Number

Children say number words while counting, or they might recognise how many objects are in a group by seeing and remembering patterns. They might chat about families and how many pets they have. Or they might notice that three dinosaurs have been left in the sand pit.

Children might sort the building blocks by shape or colour or select red cars to play with.

2. Measuring

Children can be observed seeing if the newspaper is big enough to cover the table before a craft activity. Or they might be comparing who has the biggest ball of Play-Doh.

Children might say that their birthday falls before Christmas Day or that after tidy-up, it will be story time.

3. Geometry

Children often notice the position of items. For example, their bus is in front of their friends' car or that a doll is in the car. Children frequently encounter and embrace patterns and shapes in their play. They might make a bracelet using alternate red and yellow beads or suggest they all sit in a circle to play a game.

The range of maths covered by young children in everyday play is wonderful. Do you see how it's more than knowing their numbers to ten? When teaching your baby maths, you will miss a huge opportunity if you only focus on introducing them to the first few numbers.

The days that follow address these key areas your baby will soon be engaging with.

►ACTIVITY◄

Bath fun

What a lovely time to bond with your baby and enjoy maths together—in the bathtub!

Try these ways to introduce the three key areas in the maths curriculum while in the bath:

- Number – Sing a bath song such as 'Five Little Ducks Went Swimming One Day' using rubber bath ducks to make the numbers real and visible for your baby.
- Measurement – Use plastic tippy cups to show measurement concepts such as "full" and "empty".
- Geometry – When resting your baby on your arm, use geometry words such as "up" and "down" as you lower him or her into the water and lift your little one out.

**There is more to maths than number
names and counting.
As your baby explores, notice how many varied
areas of maths you can talk about.**

DAY 31

Your Baby Can Do Addition and Subtraction

If you leave maths until your children go to school, they will start by learning numbers, then counting, and, finally, addition in the style of "one more than" and subtraction using "one less than." This is a long time to wait to experience simple addition and subtraction, especially when it has been shown that, at only six months old, babies already understand the principles involved.

Professor Andrea Berger and her team studied babies aged six to nine months. For this study[13] the babies wore special head nets studded with 128 sensors to track brain activity. While wearing the head nets, the babies watched a videotaped puppet show as their brain activity was monitored.

First, two puppets appeared and then were hidden by a screen. After that, a hand reached behind the screen and removed a puppet. Then, the screen was removed. The maths is clear here: 2-1=1. However, in this experiment, sometimes an unexpected second puppet showed up when the screen was removed. When that happened, the babies' brain activity indicated surprise. For them, 2-1=2 was not what they were expecting.

Interestingly, when they saw the wrong number of puppets, the babies' brain activity mirrored how adult brain activity processes errors. The same results were also found for addition.

If that isn't impressive enough, by the time your baby is nine months old, evidence based on a study by Professor of Psychology Koleen McCrink and Professor Karen Wynn demonstrated babies can understand 5+5=10 and 10-5=5.[14]

During the experiment, researchers showed babies several animated films depicting a group of moving rectangles. In the films presenting the addition scenario, five rectangles moved around a screen and then hid behind it. Five more rectangles followed. The movies ended with the screen moving off and showing either five or ten rectangles. The subtraction scenario followed a similar process.

In both scenarios, the babies' reactions and looking times demonstrated they were surprised by the wrong answer. That seems to mean they had a rudimentary grasp of addition and subtraction even for larger numbers.

These studies show your baby understands the concepts of addition and subtraction, which indicates that *now* is the ideal time to introduce the language that helps him or her to use this wonderful knowledge. As discussed on DAY 24, the language of maths can complicate things for school-age children, despite the fact that even infants *understand* the underlying concepts. Simple addition such as 1+1 can be communicated as "one **more than** one", "one **plus** one", "one **add** one", "one **and** one", "**double** one". Then, to get the answer, your child can be asked what the numbers **make**, **total**, **equal**, etc. How confusing!

This is where you come in. It is never too early to introduce the language of maths. Just be warned: It won't be long before you wish your baby did not understand the meaning of the word "MORE"!

When teaching babies to add and subtract, you have as many opportunities as you did for teaching them numbers and counting.

A good occasion to introduce this concept is when your baby starts enjoying finger foods. For example, the process of eating is a form of subtraction. Talk to your baby about eating peas like this: "You have five peas on your plate; take away one (baby eats a pea) and now you have four. Five minus one equals four."

To introduce a whole range of related vocabulary, pick a simple activity you do regularly such as laundry and pairing socks. Then say, "One sock (hold up a sock) plus one sock (hold up the matching sock) equals two socks."

In the curriculum, there are four ways to say + (and, add, more, plus) and five ways to say = (equals, make, sum, total, altogether). You would need to pair up 20 sets of socks to cover all the possible number sentences. Luckily, your baby produces a ready supply of washing!

►ACTIVITY◄

Sing 'Eight Fat Sausages Sizzling in a Pan'

A fun subtraction activity is to sing 'Eight Fat Sausages Sizzling in a Pan'. This simple rhyme introduces the idea of subtracting two items at a time. Use props (your fingers) and lots of enthusiasm to embed the concept of subtraction into your baby's brain.

★ ★ ★ ★ ★ ★ ★

Your baby understands addition and subtraction. Enough said!
Support this by teaching your baby the language explaining the concepts he or she already recognises.

DAY 32

Your Baby Recognises Shapes

Shapes are another area that even the most maths-phobic parents tend to be confident teaching their babies about. It turns out this is a good area to teach early in life. It has been learned that, even in the womb, an infant understands geometry, specifically shapes.[15]

Led by Professor Vincent Reid, scientists at Lancaster University found that when they projected three dots in the pattern of two eyes and a nose onto the mothers' pregnant stomachs, in the majority of cases, the foetus turned its head towards the lights. Maybe they were just drawn to the light? Actually, they did not turn with the same frequency when the pattern was altered to be a random shape. Instead, more often than not, the foetus ignored it.

This suggests that before babies have even seen a human face, they have such a strong understanding of shape that they can make decisions and actively seek information in their environment based on the positioning of three circles. Never underestimate your baby's maths ability!

When considering the topic of shapes, you will probably find it natural to use words to label two-dimensional (2D) shapes such as circles, triangles, squares, and rectangles. In your baby's first year, most likely he or she will receive more than one shape-themed gift—a shape puzzle, a colour and shape book, or a playmat with different shapes. These all work wonderfully to prompt you to use the language of shapes with your baby.

However, in real life, the vast majority of shapes your baby will encounter are actually three dimensional (3D). Even for adults, 3D shapes can be confusing. Is it a prism or a pyramid? A cube or a cuboid? In their first year of school, children are only expected to know about cubes, pyramids, spheres, and cones. Teach them these early, and they will repay the favour by teaching you about tetrahedrons, ellipsoids, and pentagonal prisms as they progress through school with the solid foundation you provided.

To truly master shapes, you need descriptive words beyond the shape's name. Help your baby understand and use words such as "flat", "curved", "straight", "solid", "face", "side", "edge", and "corner". That will enable him or her to articulate this crucial area of geometry when the time comes.

None of these words are hard for babies to understand. They do not have preconceived ideas that the word "cube" is trickier to grasp than "square" or that "sphere" is more difficult than "circle". Your baby will learn whatever you choose to teach. When you look around, you will be amazed how many shapes you can point out and name.

▶ ACTIVITY ◀

Potato painting

Today's activity is an old favourite that's been around for generations. Follow these simple steps to make beautiful paintings or wrapping paper:

1. Cut two potatoes in half.
2. On the four potato halves, cut the outline of four different shapes. On the first one, cut a square; on the next one, cut a circle; then cut a star and a triangle on the remaining pieces.
3. Cut away the top one centimetre of the potato up to the outline of the shape. You should be left with a raised shape.
4. Under careful supervision (ideally outdoors), let your baby enjoy dipping the potato shape in bowls of paint and printing shapes on the paper.
5. Chat about the printed shapes and take time to describe them to keep your baby's focus on them.

Your baby recognises shapes before birth. Amazing! Nurture this by teaching your baby key maths words to understand and describe shapes.

DAY 33

Your Baby Loves Geometry – Position and Direction

While you may not realise you have been teaching your baby maths when saying things like, "I'm going to put you **in** the car seat" or "Your toy is **behind** the cushion", you are actually introducing them to one area of geometry.

Some of these words you will use constantly with your baby from birth, and they will be among the first words your baby says. Words such as "in", "on", and "under" are among the easiest positional words for your baby. "Inside", "outside", "over", "on top", and "next to" are next to fall into conversation naturally. A little more effort may be needed when teaching your baby complex words such as "in between", "beneath", "beside", "around", "forwards", "backwards" and "sideways". And one of the trickiest maths ideas to grasp is "left" and "right".

Consider these three effective ways to introduce the vocabulary and concepts to your baby:

1. Books
2. Nursery Rhymes
3. Soft Play

1. Books

Classic stories like *We're Going on a Bear Hunt* by Michael Rosen have plenty of positional words such as "under", "over" and "through" as well as lots of repetition to cement the words. *Rosie's Walk* by Pat Hutchins is, in essence, one long sentence of about 80 words. However, despite being such a short book, it manages to fit in lots of positional words such as "across", "around", "over", "past", "through", "beside", and "under".

2. Nursery Rhymes

So many nursery rhymes have positional language in them that not only introduce your baby to vocabulary in a fun way but also encourage you to engage by incorporating actions. Consider 'The Grand Old Duke of York' rhyme. Do not only say the words "up" and "down" but lift your baby up and bounce your baby down as you sing the words. If you want to up the energy levels, then 'The Hokey Cokey' is great for whizzing your baby in, out, in, out!

3. Soft Play

Once your baby is crawling, then narrating the steps while moving ticks off a lot of positional words quickly. They will be relevant and real, because you let your baby take the lead. Expect to find yourself reeling off a plethora of positional words such as "You're **in** the tunnel", "You're **on** the slide", "The ball has rolled **behind** you", "Are you going **up** the steps?" Have a few words in mind so you can use trickier positional words in this natural setting. For example, you could say "Can you crawl **backwards** to get out?" or "Now reach your **right** hand **sideways**..."

If your baby keeps moving and you keep talking, you will be providing a wonderful language-and-maths-rich experience.

►ACTIVITY◄

Set up a baby obstacle course

Put out cushions for your baby to crawl over. If you have a box, set it up for crawling into and coming out backwards or turning around. Place toys on the other side of the cushions to tempt your baby to retrieve them.

It can be fun to crawl alongside your baby, commenting as you go. Why not finish with you being part of the obstacle course that your baby has to navigate onto or over?

This activity gives your baby exercise, improves balance, tests coordination, and provides the fun of succeeding in each part of the course. Most of all, it will provide a sensory opportunity to learn and experience positional words in a fun, hands-on, and memorable way.

Let your baby move freely, and you will have an abundance of opportunities to use positional geometry words.
Your baby will happily do movements; you just need to provide the commentary!

DAY 34

Your Baby Can See Patterns and Symmetry

Much of maths is fundamentally based on patterns, seeing connections, and putting concepts in order. It requires logic and reasoning to solve problems and make sense of the world.

It is wonderful to discover, therefore, that as young as three months old—at the point when babies cannot yet sit up or roll over—they are capable of seeing, interpreting, and using the patterns surrounding them.

Researchers have shown that three- and four-month-old infants can successfully detect visual patterns and generalise them to new sequences. For this study, [16] babies were shown patterned sequences of different dogs—e.g., an Alaskan Malamute followed by a German Shepherd then another Alaskan Malamute. This pattern of dog A, dog B, dog A was repeated for different breeds. Then the babies were shown two new dog breeds: a Terrier and a Setter. One sequence followed the previous patterns—e.g., Terrier, Setter, Terrier. The other sequence the babies were shown followed a new pattern—e.g., Terrier, Terrier, Setter. Although the dog breeds were the same in the two new scenarios, the babies noticed the difference in the pattern. This is significant, because it demonstrates that infants can learn abstract rules visually.

Is understanding patterns an important skill? Yes. Patterns help your baby predict things while providing a sense of order. In a life of new experiences and uncertainty, your baby will feel reassured by learning that, for example, a lullaby is normally followed by milk and snuggles.

People constantly rely on patterns for the simplest of tasks. The next time you pick up a bit of leftover food from the kitchen table, consider how you know it's safe to eat. Or is it? How do you even know it is food? Because your brain worked out a pattern.

Maybe you have eaten lots of biscuits in your life but have never seen a pink iced biscuit. Still, you manage to use previous patterns to deduce that "this is a biscuit that will probably taste good."

Your baby, on the other hand, might ignore the delicious pink iced biscuit (for now at least!) and, instead, is mouthing a sock pulled off his or her foot. The patterns are clear in your brain, but your baby is still figuring them out.

Why do some people seem extremely talented? Because they can see patterns that most people miss. The artists who notice shadowing and textures, the footballers who instantly process angles and velocity, the dancers who know exactly how far they can tilt their body. These are all based on patterns that happen so fast in their brains, they are not aware of them. You may have a talent for recognising a pink iced biscuit, but you are likely unaware of all the patterns you considered before deciding to pick it up and eat it!

Maths is simply another area filled with patterns. Understanding the concept of patterns will make maths easier for your baby to learn. In fact, your baby will learn an enormous amount through play: listening to the repeating patterns in music; following the natural sequence of eat, play, sleep each day; enjoying the simple patterns in stories with a start, middle, and end. Patterns abound!

►ACTIVITY◄

Butterfly symmetry

One highly distinctive pattern is symmetry. Allow your baby to enjoy symmetry by helping him or her make a painting of a butterfly. Provide a clear black outline of a butterfly and let your little one splat spots and blobs on one side of it. Then fold the painting in half to ensure the splats form a beautiful symmetrical pattern.

★ ★ ★ ★ ★ ★

Much of maths is based on patterns, connections, sequences, logic, and reasoning. Patterns help your baby predict things and provide a sense of order. They help your baby better understand the world.

DAY 35

Your Baby Can Classify and Compare

Babies need to be able to sort and compare things before they can move on to other areas of maths. It is no surprise that, as mentioned on DAY 1, it is one of the first things your baby will do—that is, classifying you as a safe person and others as strangers.

As with many areas of maths, what seems like a simple skill actually involves more understanding than you might expect. Babies learn to classify and compare in their own time, but when you understand the process and support their learning and development, they will grasp the concepts sooner and with more confidence.

Here are the five stages in learning to classify and compare:

1. **Identifying and describing attributes:** Babies start by noticing the attributes of a particular object. From there, they need to develop the language that helps them explain their thinking. Identifying attributes requires your baby to be able to notice details and be observant. You can help by pointing out features that make items similar or different.

2. **Matching:** For this stage, it is not enough to only identify different attributes. Your baby needs to focus on the *sameness* of an attribute. A matching activity nurtures

your baby's reasoning skills, a skill commonly used in IQ tests. Your baby is little, so you would expect him or her to be able to match obvious attributes (e.g., if you show two pictures of identical yellow flowers and a picture of a house, babies are more likely to grasp that the flowers match). For older children or adults doing IQ tests, they might be shown pictures of three seemingly identical flowers, but one has an extra leaf. You can see how the underlying skills used are the same and will remain useful throughout their lives.

3. **Sorting:** This goes a step beyond matching as you help your baby group different objects with one or more attributes. Sorting involves making a variety of different decisions. The ability to sort using two or more attributes requires higher order thinking.

4. **Comparing:** It won't be long before your baby can intuitively make comparisons based on size and decisions based on the amount of an attribute two objects hold. This skill involves being engaged with determining which object possesses more or less of an attribute. To manage this, your baby needs to develop his or her vocabulary of comparative descriptions as well as an understanding that comparing is relative to the situation and that an object's description can change depending on what it is compared with. To help with this, keep using "er" words such as "longer", "heavier", and so on.

5. **Ordering:** Babies are only able to order items when they can identify and describe attributes, notice differences,

and make comparisons. Ordering involves arranging objects according to increasing or decreasing amounts of an attribute. Make sure you use "est" words such as "longest", "heaviest", and so on.

A study conducted at the Oxford BabyLab, led by Nadja Althaus, researched the effects of labelling on category learning,[17] specifically whether hearing similar words for similar objects helps facilitate a baby's ability to categorise.

In Althaus's study, 12-month-olds were shown eight images of made-up objects formed from leaves and shells. The shells varied, but the leaves remained similar. As well as seeing the images, half the babies also heard the name for them: "timbo". The study found that babies who heard the name were learning more about the object by looking at the leaves. That signifies they were able to focus on the similarities between these new objects. What is the implication? Stating a name while viewing an object helps babies find similarities between different objects. For example, when they hear you say "dog" they compare a particular dog with their neighbours' dog or the dog they saw yesterday, and then they consider what features link these animals. What an impressive skill to acquire before your baby can even talk!

Remember, the more descriptions you provide, the more detail your baby has to work with to make sense of all the new things being seen and experienced.

►ACTIVITY◄

Comparing toys

Select two toys and, with your baby, compare them to each other. Have on hand additional toys that reinforce the features you are discussing. For example, you could start by comparing a red cube and a yellow cube. Point out they are both cubes and hold up a third cube to also demonstrate what a cube is. Mention they are different colours and then find another red toy and another yellow toy to highlight which aspect of the cube you are referring to as you talk about its colour. Let your baby play with the items as you discuss them. If he or she picks up the yellow cube, then this is where the focus is, so describe *all* its features at that point. You might say, "That is a yellow **cube**. Look, it's **bigger** than the red **cube** and the blue **cube**. Wow, it is the **biggest cube**!"

★ ★ ★ ★ ★ ★ ★

Identify, match, sort, compare, and order.
That's a lot for your baby to understand!
Help babies describe the objects they are
interested in by teaching them the names.

DAY 36

Your Baby Recognises the Importance of Size

From as young as ten months old, babies seem to have a grasp of relative size.

A study led by Professor Lotte Thomsen[18] showed ten-month-old babies videos that featured a large and a small block with eyes and mouth crossing the stage, one from each side. When they met in the middle, the babies saw either the large or the small block allow the other past. The babies looked for twice as long when the large block gave way to the small block. This demonstrated they were surprised by this action.

This becomes interesting because the babies understood the fundamental difference between the blocks was their relative size. It seems they were then able to process this abstract scenario, understand it, and compare it to real-life events on which their expectations had been shaped. It should be noted that the younger eight-month-olds did not respond in the same way; they failed to grasp the significance of size.

When your baby can perceive the difference in size of objects and can predict actions based on this information, it helps to provide the maths vocabulary to label the concepts. That's why you want to describe them out loud.

►ACTIVITY◄

Big to small

For today's activity, emphasise the sequence of events when something goes from big to small or from small to big. For example, when chopping up a banana for your baby, you could explain the sequence this way:

1. "We start with this **big** piece of banana. Is it too **big** for you? Shall we cut it into **small** bits?"
2. "That's **one** chop. Now it's **half** the size, and there are **two small** pieces instead of **one big** piece."
3. "Now, it's time to eat the banana. Would you like to eat the **small** pieces? Would you like them to be **smaller**?"

You will notice this one short, everyday exchange includes an impressive quantity of maths vocabulary.

★ ★ ★ ★ ★ ★

Your baby understands that some objects are big and others are small. Not only that, he or she can make logical assumptions based on this information. Wow!

DAY 37

Your Baby Grasps the Concept of Time

Does your baby understand the concept of time? As you're awakened at 2 am, it feels like the answer to this is a resounding "no". And in some ways, you would be right.

However, at one month old, it has been shown that babies do develop a primitive sense of time, which means you should start to see a difference in your baby's day and night routines.

What's more, in 1969, Dr Hiram E Fitzgerald, University Distinguished Professor in the Department of Psychology, Michigan State University, carried out an interesting study.[19] In this study, babies were taught a 20-second time interval by having a light switched on every 20 seconds while they were in a dark room. After this initial teaching phase, they then repeated the experiment without turning on the lights. Researchers discovered that every 20 seconds, the babies' pupils still constricted in anticipation of the light coming on.

Once again, the science shows how much your baby can be taught. Your job is to support this by explaining and providing words and scenarios so he or she better understands what is happening in the world.

Time can be seen as a tricky area of maths. Many different concepts are needed to understand telling the time using an analogue clock. Not the least of these concepts is knowing the five times table in order to calculate how many minutes have passed. It is not easy when your child sees the long hand pointing at the number four for them to remember that five times four is 20 (5 x 4 = 20), so it must be 20 minutes past the hour.

While days of the week are another seemingly abstract notion to babies, it helps to get them used to the names of each day and their order. *Cookie's Week* by Cindy Ward is great for this.

Regardless of whether time is tricky or not, your baby will thrive on knowing what is likely to happen next. Most babies love routine and structure, which works well for teaching time concepts. Even at a young age, you can talk to your baby about what you are doing now or later. You might divide your baby's day into morning, afternoon, and evening while clearly defining bedtime, playtime, and dinnertime. Use consistent markers to show what is coming next; for example, wash hands before dinnertime or change into night-time clothes before bed.

The national curriculum maths vocabulary for the topic of time is broad and covers areas such as:

* seasons: spring, summer, autumn, winter
* month, year, weekend
* birthday, holiday, morning, afternoon, evening, bedtime, dinner time, playtime
* today, yesterday, tomorrow, before, after, next, last, now, soon, early, late
* quick, quicker, quickest, quickly, fast, faster, fastest, slow, slower, slowest, slowly
* old, older, oldest, new, newer, newest, takes longer, takes less time
* hour, o'clock, half past, clock, watch, hands
* always, never, often, sometimes, usually

As you can see, you have a lot of words to introduce, so the sooner the better!

Remember, any discussion about time and routines will not only help your baby but will also help you pass your busy days without them becoming a chaotic blur.

►ACTIVITY◄

Sing a days of the week song

Every Week

Every week has seven days,

See how many you can say.

Sunday, Monday, Tuesday, Wednesday, Thursday, Friday, Saturday.

What's today?

When sung often enough, this short song will tick off nine time-related maths words.

★ ★ ★ ★ ★ ★

Understanding the concept of time can be tricky for anyone. Introducing your baby to the wide variety of time-related maths vocabulary will pay dividends and might provide needed structure to your day.

6

BABY MATHS CLASSES

"You cannot make people learn. You can only provide the right conditions for learning to happen."

– VINCE GOWMON,
author, *Let the Fire Burn: Nurturing the Creative Spirit of Children*

DAY 38

Baby Maths Classes Overview

As a parent, you will be deluged with an overwhelming range of "essential" toys, books, activities, and classes that promise to give your baby that sought-after head start. You might be forgiven for thinking that baby maths classes are a step too far down the hot-housing route. As it happens, there does not actually seem to be much in the way of pure maths classes for babies.

Would having maths classes for babies be good? Absolutely! Maths is an essential life skill and confidence—or, more commonly, anxiety—can be built in the first few formative years.

So, if baby maths classes aren't readily available, what is the solution? As luck would have it, a whole range of alternative baby classes are offered. What you may not realise is that any of them can introduce your baby to the wonderful, fascinating, powerful world of maths in its own fun way. You just need to understand how to tailor the classes near you to meet your baby's maths development needs. Simple!

If you are not sure how to turn your local baby class into maths exploration, the next few days point out how several popular classes can be used to nurture your baby's maths confidence and ability.

To get results, it is not necessary to immerse your baby in maths in a rigid, pre-prepared way; any time invested will benefit your baby. Just take your baby's lead, follow his or her eye line, and talk about whatever interests him or her. Be prepared; interests will change constantly!

Classes in general help with bonding and promoting a secure attachment. The class structure introduces your baby to routines and, therefore, sequences and patterns—both important aspects of mathematics. And while baby classes are designed to be fun and keep your baby engaged, focusing on set activities in a group gradually helps increase your baby's attention span and ability to concentrate—key skills for future maths learning in a structured school environment.

Pick any class that you and your baby would enjoy. And embrace the fact that maths is present in every activity, making it particularly easy to teach your baby maths.

▶ A C T I V I T Y ◀

Balloon play

Tie two helium balloons to your baby's feet, let him or
her kick freely, and watch the excitement. This is a simple,
enjoyable activity that would not be out of place in a sensory
baby class or a baby gym class.

Does this really teach your baby maths? Think back to
DAY 30 and the areas of maths. It pointed out three key
areas that are most relevant at this age. Do these activities
to cover each of the areas in one simple activity:

1. Number – Count the two balloons or the number of
    leg kicks.
2. Measurement – Use words like "big" balloon, "long"
    string, "high" kicks.
3. Geometry – For the properties of shapes, say that the
    balloons are nearly spherical and, for position, see the
    legs and balloons go up and down.

★ ★ ★ ★ ★ ★

Maths is everywhere!
Any baby class can be a baby maths class.

DAY 39

Baby Music Classes

Because music is so loved by babies, chances are you are spoilt with the range and availability of baby music classes. Most libraries hold a free weekly rhyme time session and there are also lots of other music classes aimed at babies. But how exactly does music teach your baby maths?

For one thing, you can use music to introduce your baby to numeracy by singing number rhymes. Everyone knows it's easier to learn a catchy song than memorise a dry list of facts, so use this to help your baby learn the number names. In addition, by rattling instruments, bouncing, and hearing music, your baby will be introduced to mathematical concepts such as timing, fractions, counting, and opposites—fast and slow, loud and quiet, high and low.

Music, like maths, is full of patterns. Music generally has a clear structure with a repeating rhythm and a regular beat, making it a natural way to introduce maths to your baby. And babies love music!

►ACTIVITY◄

Take or create a baby music class

Go to a local music class or have friends with babies come around and create your own class. To reinforce the maths concepts, count the beats as you bounce the babies. As you do, take time to explain what they are hearing using mathematical language and gestures. For example, if a song had the word "up", then you'd lift your babies up.

★ ★ ★ ★ ★ ★ ★

Music is everywhere, and music
is full of maths.
Teaching music will automatically boost your
baby's maths ability.

DAY 40

Baby Massage and Yoga

Did you know that babies are born with an ability to perform complex yoga moves?

Both baby yoga and baby massage come with a host of benefits such as the promise of improved sleeping patterns, help with digestion and constipation, and relief for gas and colic. And clearly, they provide great bonding opportunities. The soothing techniques of massage will teach you to help your baby calm himself or herself. They also increase body awareness, both for you and your baby.

Doing yoga is a great way to strengthen your body, calm your mind and feel relaxed. This, in turn, can lead to reduced stress for you and your baby. And it is something the two of you can continue long beyond the baby years. Healthy habits learned early in life become healthy habits later in life.

These are compelling reasons to attend classes, but what about learning maths? You likely won't see baby massage or baby yoga classes advertise how they will maximise your baby's maths ability—a missed opportunity for sure. However, notice these three key mathematical elements to baby massage and yoga:

1. The process of including a series of massage or yoga moves in your baby's routine introduces the idea of sequences.
2. Special one-to-one activities help you bond with your baby and comfort him or her. More than that, forming a secure attachment has been linked to an increase in intelligence test scores.
3. As with any movement-related activity, the maths language can flow. For example, you can count strokes and talk about massaging **up** or **down** the **left** leg or **right** leg. You might move your hand round in a **circle**. Be sure to add maths vocabulary to any action you make.

Simple baby massage techniques can be used at any time of the day. For example, you can add massage to the nappy change routine, as part of drying your baby after a bath, or at any point when your baby needs extra attention.

Consider specific routines and techniques that can ease certain conditions. For example, gently rubbing your baby's tummy in a clockwise motion can help ease gas, colic, or constipation. Perhaps attend a baby massage group to learn additional movements or search for video tutorials online.

Massaging your baby's legs can be a good place to start because babies are used to being touched there during nappy changes. It is an easy area to access without your baby getting cold from having too many layers removed. The movements are good for your baby's circulation, muscle tone, and skin condition. And most babies love having their legs massaged.

Gently stroke down both legs, applying oil or cream if you choose. As you massage, keep talking and engaging with your baby with statements such as "**First**, I am going to massage your **right** leg from **top** to **bottom**." Notice how many maths words are in this simple sentence. Your baby will love the gentle motion of the massage combined with your soothing voice.

There are many lovely massage techniques you can slowly incorporate. Each one introduces the idea of sequencing, routines, and patterns, as well as the constant flow of mathematical language.

What a great way to teach your baby maths!

►ACTIVITY◄

Introduce your baby to yoga

Why not also include a yoga move in your bonding time today? To introduce the yoga position Downward Dog, lay your baby over your legs and gently raise your knees so tummy time on mummy becomes a relaxing yoga stretch. Count while holding the pose to teach your baby maths as you gently stretch your baby's back while enjoying tummy time in a fun way.

Both massage and yoga are wonderful ways of teaching your baby maths while boosting other areas of development and bonding.

★ ★ ★ ★ ★ ★ ★

Soothing sequences set the scene for introducing your baby to maths-rich language while bonding through relaxing massages and yoga moves.

DAY 41

Baby Craft Classes

A lot of parents understandably shy away from messy play at home, especially during the first year when the mess-to-results ratio is frankly not encouraging. Luckily, plenty of baby groups have a craft table set up and some are entirely focused on messy play.

The joy of craft sessions is that your baby can experience the maths vocabulary you have been introducing. If they are sticking, painting, or ripping, then talk about the shapes and sizes. If they are tipping, washing, or pouring, then talk about measurements. How full is the pot of paint? How wide is their painting? If they are squishing, stretching, or separating dough, then count the pieces, compare the lengths, and make different shapes. Do all this together as you make maths real and fun for your baby.

►ACTIVITY◄

Paper ripping

It is not clear why, but babies seem to love watching paper rip. They also enjoy joining in with the destruction. To begin with, babies grab both ends of the paper in their fists and pull. As their dexterity and strength increase, they will be able to hold the paper with their fingers rather than their fists and tear off more precise strips.

Not only is this fun for babies, it also builds hand strength, hand-eye coordination, precision, and bilateral coordination. It teaches them the tripod grip and helps them develop the muscles used for writing—an all-round super activity.

But where does the maths come in? As you play, talk about how many strips have been ripped, what size they are, and if they broke in half or quarters. By nine months, your baby should be happily tearing paper. If your baby is under nine months old, then just watching you will elicit a huge amount of enjoyment!

★ ★ ★ ★ ★ ★ ★

Messy play can be mathsy play!
Embrace the crafts and the chaos—let your
baby lead the maths exploration.

DAY 42

Baby Sensory Classes

Baby sensory classes focus on engaging all your baby's senses. They provide creative play, massage, tummy time, movement, and visual development as well as introduce different textures, a variety of scents, and simple music in structured ways.

You may think these classes offer such a range of new experiences purely to keep your baby entertained. However, involving babies in sensory experiences from birth advances their development significantly—an important benefit. Stimulating infants with different textures, sights, sounds, smells, and tastes boosts their intelligence and understanding of the world around them.

You can use individual sensory activities to teach your baby maths. Examples are getting a massage, seeing a parachute waft up and down, hearing number songs and nursery rhymes, playing with bubbles, learning sign language, and experimenting with age-appropriate toys such as chunky jigsaw puzzles. The maths benefits of each of these activities are detailed elsewhere in this book.

In general, the more babies use their senses, the more concepts in maths will become real and memorable. When they grasp different objects and find that some fit in the puzzle and others do not, they begin to understand the concept of bigger and smaller. When you see them mouthing a toy, they are learning about its weight, size, shape, and texture. When they see a tower of blocks fall, they are observing real-life maths in action.

All these experiences provide the building blocks to not only better understand and apply maths as they grow older, but also build in the knowledge that maths is fun and relevant.

▶ ᴀᴄᴛɪᴠɪᴛʏ ◀

Jelly painting

Seek a baby class that focuses on engaging all your baby's senses, then sign up for a taster class. Or even treat your baby to sensory play at home. For example, try painting with jelly. The sweet smell will make the activity inviting, and your baby will love squidging the jelly in his or her hands. You can count the jelly blobs with your baby as they are created. The colour of the circular jelly blobs will show up on white paper as you let your baby have fun smearing it. This "painting" gives you a lasting memento of this fun activity.

The best bit? Your baby also engages in his or her sense of taste!

★ ★ ★ ★ ★ ★ ★

It's a simple fact that the more senses your baby engages when exploring new things, the more memorable any new experiences will be. Use this to introduce your baby to maths in an unforgettable sensory journey of discovery.

DAY 43

Baby Gym Classes

On DAY 33, you saw how movement can be a great way to introduce positional geometry vocabulary to your baby. Baby gym classes encourage your baby to move safely in a fun, age-appropriate environment. A lot of baby gym classes are held in halls where they have access to baby-safe slopes, steps, and slides for exploring.

These soft-obstacle courses are excellent for physical development and equally beneficial for teaching maths vocabulary. They allow babies to enjoy rolling **down** slopes as well as sliding **on** their tummies, moving **backwards**, crawling **through** tunnels, and climbing **in**, **out**, **up**, and **over** things. The classes also encourage babies who are not yet mobile to have fun with activities that strengthen their bodies in preparation for movement. These include rocking, rolling, standing, pull ups, and tummy time. They might also use props such as ribbons, beanbags, hula hoops, scarves, maracas, and bells to support and encourage varied movements.

You will find that bending, stretching, jumping, turning, shaking, wiggling, stamping, clapping, and swinging are all wonderful not only for your baby's physical development but also for understanding maths. The movement develops your baby's spatial awareness and helps with bilateral coordination or movements that cross the midline. Bilateral coordination refers to the ability to use both sides of the body together. Activities such as crawling, climbing a ladder or playing the drums are important because they require both sides of the brain to work together to coordinate the body's movements.

Interestingly, studies have identified a link between reduced movement in infancy and academic delays. For example, a study by the Institute for Neuro-Physiological Psychology[20] found that nearly a third of four- and five-year-olds could not do basic physical movements such as crawling or standing on one leg. This deficiency also seemed to link to poor academic achievement. The research found that, of the pupils in the bottom half of the group for physical maturity, 77 percent were also in the lowest two groups for academic ability.

In general, babies today are being carried more than in the past, and their time in front of a screen has increased. This has resulted in less movement and less tummy time where their key muscles and skills develop.

Do you see how important movement is for your baby? If introducing the language of maths encourages movement, that can only be a good thing.

►ACTIVITY◄

Rock your baby on a ball

In a local baby gym class or a soft play group, let your baby enjoy the freedom of movement, knowing it will boost his or her maths ability, too. For an at-home activity, place your baby tummy down on a big exercise ball and, holding your baby carefully, roll the ball slightly forwards and backwards while singing the pirate song 'When I Was One, I Sucked My Thumb the Day I Went to Sea'. Emphasise the maths words "forwards" and "backwards" when you get to the chorus.

Tummy time is an extremely important aspect of child development that will help your baby strengthen the muscles required for rolling, sitting, reaching, pivoting, and crawling. Not all babies initially love being placed on their tummies. This activity not only fits nicely with introducing maths vocabulary, but it also makes tummy time more exciting for your baby.

Movement is good for your baby's physical
and cognitive development.
Make comments as your baby moves, and the
NUMBER TALK will naturally flow.

MATHS BOOSTS ALL AREAS OF DEVELOPMENT

"Without mathematics, there's nothing you can do. Everything around you is mathematics. Everything around you is numbers."

– SHAKUNTALA DEVI,
mathematician known as the "Human Computer"

DAY 44

Maths Boosts All Areas of
Development Overview

The first few years of your baby's life will whizz by, with feeds, sleep, and nappy changes absorbing a lot of time. A common concern for parents is not having enough time to also teach their baby maths.

This book aims to show that squeezing maths activities into your baby's life need not occur to the detriment of other areas of development.

It is useful that the Department of Education published the revised *Statutory Framework for the Early Years Foundation Stage* in March 2014. It makes it mandatory for all schools, nurseries, and childminders caring for children from birth to five years old to ensure all areas of infant development are covered. Devised by child development experts, this Framework offers a huge number of excellent suggestions.

Its baby curriculum, a valuable resource, highlights these six areas of learning and development for infants:

1. Personal, social, and emotional development
   a) making relationships
   b) self-confidence and self-awareness
   c) managing feelings and behaviour

2. Communication and language
   a) listening and attention
   b) understanding
   c) speaking

3. Physical development
   a) moving and handling
   b) health and self-care

4. Literacy
5. Mathematics
6. Understanding the world

Unfortunately, maths doesn't receive much emphasis. In fact, when analysing the nearly 100 suggested activities aimed at babies from birth to 11 months, only nine are listed under the mathematics heading.

Does this mean that maths is not important for babies? Clearly, this is not the case. Will teaching your baby maths take valuable time away from other areas of development? Absolutely not.

The fantastic thing about teaching your baby maths is that it need *not* detract from other areas. If specifically teaching your baby maths helps you to engage more actively, then you will be improving all areas of your little one's development. Far from *detracting* from other areas of growth, teaching your baby maths *improves* them.

To better understand this premise, let's look at the activities suggested in the curriculum guidance material. This will be covered area by area over the next few days. You will be guided to teach your baby maths using the activities suggested from each of the different areas of development. In that way, you can learn how easily maths fits in with every aspect of your baby's life.

Amazingly, teaching your baby maths ends up ticking many developmental boxes! By investing your time interacting positively with your baby, you will automatically boost your communication. This leads to better literacy skills and improved understanding of the world he or she lives in.

Additionally, any time spent with your baby will help with personal, social, and emotional development. Whether you are chatting, playing, reading a story, or just holding your baby, you communicate that you are there for him or her. In the important formative first months, what your baby needs most is *you* and *your attention*.

▶ ACTIVITY ◀

Baby maths curriculum suggestions

Before looking at the other areas of development and how teaching your baby maths can add to them, read what the *Statutory Framework for the Early Years Foundation Stage* suggests specifically to help with your baby's maths development. Here are three suggestions for you to enjoy with your baby today.

- *Sing number rhymes as you dress or change babies, e.g., 'One, Two, Buckle My Shoe'.*
- *Encourage babies to join in tapping and clapping along to simple rhythms.*
- *Collect number rhymes which are repetitive and are related to children's actions and experiences, for example, 'Peter Hammers with One Hammer'.*

(Excerpt from *Development Matters in the Early Years Foundation Stage Guidance* – Mathematics: Numbers p32)

Teaching your baby maths does not *detract* from other areas of development—it *boosts* them.

DAY 45

Personal, Social, and Emotional Development

Making Relationships

The importance of personal, social, and emotional development for babies is reflected in the fact that one third of all suggestions in the *Statutory Framework for the Early Years Foundation Stage* relate to this area.

Within the *Statutory Framework*, personal, social, and emotional development is subdivided into Making Relationships, Self-confidence and Self-awareness, and Managing Feelings and Behaviour. Today focuses on Making Relationships.

In our culture, it often seems that babies do not need to be taught how to engage socially. With just one giggle or the hint of a cry, they have people around them totally absorbed. Do not forget that babies' intuitive maths skills enable them to understand cause and effect at a base level—that is, they cry, they get attention, and their needs are addressed.

Sadly, if your baby is taught there is no cause-and-effect relationship and crying does not elicit the needed help, certain neurological pathways will be pruned, and your baby will not fully develop socially or emotionally.

If your baby is a socially and emotionally developed infant, then he or she will enjoy the company of others from birth, responding by gazing at faces and copying facial movements when talked to.

Using the maths skill of categorising people, your baby will be most responsive to your voice. Likely when you appear, his or her face will brighten, and activity will increase. It is good to realise your baby will naturally follow your gaze and pay attention to whatever appears important to you.

As you know, your baby loves cuddling and being held, feeling calm in your arms, or just snuggling, smiling, gazing at your face, and even stroking your skin.

Unsurprisingly, the activities under this heading mostly relate to attachment and interaction. The great thing is, they can easily be achieved while calmly enjoying one-to-one maths-related activities.

The more time you spend interacting with your baby, the better you will understand what he or she needs. Follow your baby's lead—talk about what he or she is looking at or eating, count the poppers on their Babygro, etc.—then teaching your baby maths will help you sensitively tune in to your baby.

►ACTIVITY◄

Plan one-to-one time

Today and over the next few days, the activities to teach your baby maths will be taken directly from the *Statutory Framework* for the relevant developmental area. Thereby, demonstrating that teaching your baby maths boosts all areas of development.

"Plan to have one-to-one time to interact with young babies when they are in an alert and responsive state and willing to engage."

(Excerpt from *Development Matters in the Early Years Foundation Stage Guidance* –Personal, Social and Emotional Development: Making Relationships p8)

You can use one-to-one maths time to sing a number song, read a shapes book, count ducks, massage your baby, etc. while also boosting his or her relationship-making skills.

All the maths suggestions in this book require you to spend quality time with your baby, thereby enhancing his or her personal, social, and emotional development. There need be no compromises when allocating time to teaching your baby maths.

Boost your baby's personal, social, and emotional development through one-to-one time exploring maths together.

DAY 46

Personal, Social and Emotional Development

Self-Confidence and Self-Awareness

If your baby is confident and self-aware, he or she will be relaxed, most likely laughing and gurgling while showing pleasure during physical interactions such as being tickled or rocked. Your baby will also feel at ease using his or her voice, gestures, eye contact, and facial expressions while making contact with others and keeping their attention.

This hugely important area of development is simple to achieve by taking time to show pleasure in being with your baby. You want to be close by and available. Most importantly, you want to make sure your baby feels safe and loved even when he or she cannot be at the centre of your attention.

By helping your baby develop self-confidence and self-awareness, you are building a special, loving relationship in which your baby knows you will respond positively when interacting with you. This benefits your baby and also helps with teaching maths.

If babies know you will interact with them, they often lead the teaching by crawling to their favourite number book. They already trust you will take time to enjoy it with them. By holding up a flower, they feel confident you will talk to them about it, count the petals, point to the shapes, and engage with them. Again, they know you will enjoy it with them.

►ACTIVITY◄

Respond to your baby's expressions

"Respond to and build on babies' expressions, actions, and gestures. Babies will repeat actions that get a positive response from you."

(Excerpt from *Development Matters in the Early Years Foundation Stage Guidance* – Personal, Social and Emotional Development: Self-confidence and Self-awareness p10)

This activity is an ideal way to teach your baby about the maths area of patterns and taking turns. As he or she pulls a face, for example, you respond. It really is as easy as that to build your baby's self-confidence, self-awareness, *and* maths ability.

★ ★ ★ ★ ★ ★ ★

**Teaching maths should be led by your baby
and be spontaneous in nature.
Your baby's self-confidence and self-awareness
build when you engage with him or her.**

DAY 47

Personal, Social and Emotional Development

Managing Feelings and Behaviour

Typically, babies should feel comforted by their parents' touch, faces, and voices. They should seek physical and emotional comfort by snuggling with them and other trusted adults. After being upset, they should calm down when parents hold them, rock them, speak or sing to them with soothing voices. Babies should show a range of emotions such as pleasure, fear, and excitement. They should also react to other people's emotions, smiling back when smiled at as an example. And it would be normal for them to feel distress if they hear another baby crying.

All of these feelings and behaviours can be expected from your baby in the first year—*if* he or she is able to manage them. Be alert to ways you can nurture those feelings and behaviours through your baby's first year and beyond.

►ACTIVITY◄

Sing 'Twinkle, Twinkle Little Star'

"Use calming processes such as rocking or hugging."

(Excerpt from *Development Matters in the Early Years Foundation Stage Guidance* –
Personal, Social and Emotional Development: Managing feelings and behaviour p12)

To teach your baby maths today, sing 'Twinkle, Twinkle Little Star'—a soothing lullaby that includes the maths vocabulary of "little", "up", "above", "diamond", "star", and "in". Sing before nap time while gently rocking or hugging him or her to sleep. Investing quality time teaching your baby maths with a goodnight song will also boost your loved one's ability to manage his or her feelings and behaviour.

Focusing on your baby while enjoying maths activities means being present, engaged, and ready to provide comfort and soothing when needed. Teaching your baby maths means you will be there for your baby.

DAY 48

Communication and Language

Listening and Attention

Much of the process of teaching your baby maths rests on introducing your baby in a fun, engaging way to the *language* of maths. Essential to the process is removing the mystery of what can seem like tricky words by using them frequently and enthusiastically during your baby's early years. No new maths vocabulary is actually tricky for your baby. However, examples of words that some parents shy away from using in conversation during the first year are "sphere" and "symmetrical". It can take extra effort to use words like this, but it is worth it.

To absorb the language of maths, it is key that your baby develops good listening and attention skills. Teaching your baby maths using the activities throughout this book will, in fact, also improve his or her ability to listen and pay attention. Win, win!

In their first year, babies typically turn towards familiar sounds and accurately locate them. They should listen to, distinguish, and respond to the sounds and intonations of voices. They should show reactions when interacting with others by smiling, looking, and moving. In addition, they should become quiet and alert when they hear speech.

Based on typical ways for babies to communicate, you can expect your baby to look intently at you as you talk but stop responding if you turn away. However, be prepared for your baby to have a fleeting attention span. This is not under your baby's control; any new stimuli will absorb his or her whole attention.

In short, your baby loves listening to you but prefers to have your undivided attention. What should you do? Focus fully on your baby during activities that teach maths while you state what is happening! This will improve your baby's listening, attention, and maths under-standing all in one go.

Activities included under this area of the *Statutory Framework*—turn-taking, peek-a-boo, rhymes and so on—may have been written by the British Association of Early Childhood Education to teach babies listening and attention skills but they all actually also provide the perfect type of activities to teach your baby maths (as detailed elsewhere throughout this book).

Feel confident knowing that when you invest your precious time teaching your baby maths, you are also boosting other areas of development. That can be highly motivating.

►ACTIVITY◄

Play patty cake

"Encourage playfulness, turn-taking and responses, including peek-a-boo and rhymes."

(Excerpt from *Development Matters in the Early Years Foundation Stage Guidance* – Communication and Language: Listening and Attention p15)

For a new activity that teaches your baby maths while encouraging playfulness, turn-taking, and rhyming, introduce "patty cake" today. This fun clapping game involves rhythm, coordination, repetition, and understanding of patterns. It also helps develop your baby's logical thinking.

Primarily, you are teaching your baby maths with this activity. Here's the bonus: it will also boost your loved one's listening and attention skills.

★ ★ ★ ★ ★ ★ ★

Teaching your baby maths through fun games and other activities will also boost listening and attention skills.
No need to choose which area of development to focus on; every area will benefit.

DAY 49

Communication and Language

Understanding

A vast body of scientific research confirms the importance of simply talking to your baby. That evidence is impossible to ignore; there's no longer any doubt that babies understand a lot of what is said to them.

You can expect your baby to quickly learn to stop and look when hearing his or her name. Your baby will also begin to understand contextual clues such as words, sounds, and familiar gestures. If you believe babies understand what you are telling them, that makes the time spent teaching your baby maths more engaging for both you and your baby.

Time and again, this book emphasises communicating with your baby. The suggested daily maths activities include ideas for stepping up your regular communication. In this way, maths need not be seen as an abstract.

Be conscious that no sentence you say will only teach your baby maths. Instead, you engage with your baby while helping him or her make sense of the surrounding world. Communication, like maths, is key for every area of development.

Often, communication naturally involves maths. For example, the dog babies point at is "big"; the door they point at is a "rectangle"; the cuddle they reach for is "up"; the food they point at is "more". It is amazing how maths plays a part in everything!

►ACTIVITY◄

Give meaning to the things your baby points at

"Interpret and give meaning to the things young babies show interest in, e.g., when babies point to an object, tell them what it is."

(Excerpt from *Development Matters in the Early Years Foundation Stage Guidance* – Communication and Language: Understanding p17)

Sometimes just being aware of the language of maths can open whole new lines of communication. Today, follow your baby's gaze or point and talk about whatever interests him or her. Yes, today's activity is based on the curriculum guidance to teach babies communication, but it is also the "N" in NUMBER TALK: Name what you see. Use maths vocabulary as you talk. As you teach your baby maths, you are boosting their understanding of communication and language by *simply talking to them.*

★ ★ ★ ★ ★ ★

As you talk to your baby to teach maths, realise that in the process, you're teaching much more.

DAY 50

Communication and Language

Speaking

What could be more rewarding than hearing your baby's first few words and getting an insight into what he or she thinks?

In their first year, babies communicate their needs and feelings in a variety of ways, including crying, gurgling, babbling, and squealing. They also communicate with actions such as lifting their arms when they want to be picked up. They practise and practise and gradually develop speech sounds such as "baba", "nono", "gogo"—words they will use to communicate with you.

Revel in your baby's achievement when he or she communicates maths understanding—for example, lifting arms for "up" or waving and saying "bye" to indicate an understanding of the sequence of common events.

At every stage of this effort, be sure to communicate back so your baby feels listened to and encouraged to keep trying.

►ACTIVITY◄

Imitate baby's babbling in turn-taking conversations

"Encourage babies' sounds and babbling by copying their sounds in a turn-taking 'conversation'."

(Excerpt from *Development Matters in the Early Years Foundation Stage Guidance* – Communication and Language: Speaking p19)

Some of your baby's first words such as "up", "more", and "one" are key maths vocabulary.

Try to understand what babies are striving to communicate by being engaged in the conversation and repeating back what they might be trying to express. For example, if they bang the table or reach out towards the packet of food and say "momo", , you could respond with "**More**? Would you like **more**? Here is **more** food."

Turn-taking, copying your baby's babbling, encouraging your little one's first sounds—these are intuitive and natural responses when encouraging your baby to *talk*. It's a small step to then use the same instincts to teach your baby the language of maths.

DAY 51

Physical Development

Moving and Handling

This is arguably the most measured and compared area of infant development. Even years into the future, people will ask when your baby first walked.

Physical development is hugely important for babies. In their first year, they roll, lift their heads, sit, reach for items, hold them, and even transfer them from one hand to the other. You never know, your baby might even take those exciting first steps. All physical development milestones are fascinating to witness.

The question is, will teaching your baby maths slow down the rate at which your baby physically develops? Of course not.

DAY 33 looked at the maths area of position and movement language. Teaching your baby about this area of geometry involves lots of wonderful physical actions: ups and downs, lefts and rights, fasts and slows, ins and outs. In fact, it would be almost impossible to teach your baby maths and not also improve his or her physical development.

►ACTIVITY◄

Allow your baby to move, roll, stretch, and explore

"Have well-planned areas that allow babies maximum space to move, roll, stretch and explore."

(Excerpt from *Development Matters in the Early Years Foundation Stage Guidance* – Physical Development: Movement and Handling p22)

You will be driven to provide this whether you plan to or not. Your baby simply wants to get moving. So embrace it and teach maths as you chat as your baby pulls "up" and falls "down".

Teaching maths should only encourage and boost this area of development. If parents were tempted to wedge their babies in a highchair and repeatedly test them with flashcards for hours day after day, then maths tuition could hinder their physical development. However, you'll never find a suggestion like that in this book!

★ ★ ★ ★ ★ ★ ★

Your baby's movements can flow as
the NUMBER TALK flows.
Maths and movement go hand in hand.

DAY 52

Physical Development

Health and Self-Care

When considering your baby's physical development, it is easy to focus only on his or her movement, but also pay attention to health and self-care.

In their first year, you can anticipate babies responding to and thriving on your sensitive physical contact and care. Bonding moments such as dressing, nappy changes, and bath times are great opportunities to gently talk to your baby while caring for him or her. Count the poppers on the vest **one**, **two**, **three**. Lift your baby's **right** leg and then **left** leg. Tip the water **on** as you lift your baby's head **up**. You get the idea!

Babies also express discomfort, hunger, and thirst as they learn to anticipate food routines with interest. The more familiar your baby becomes with the key maths-area of sequences, the less anxiety he or she will feel waiting for the next step in the routine.

How can you support this development? By gradually allowing your baby to share control of the food and drink, have regular feeding patterns, and be aware of individual cues.

You can also establish an overall routine that includes many elements of self-care—from teeth brushing to regular feeding. This helps maintain a structure that supports thriving in this important area of physical development.

Teach your baby the maths areas of time and sequences by creating a daily routine poster. Think about the main elements of your day (e.g., wake up, breakfast, play, nap, lunch, etc.). You can include activities you would like to do regularly, such as story time, massage, rhyme time, and other maths activity time. It can be useful to put Velcro tabs on your daily routine poster so you can swap activity pictures. Perhaps on Mondays, you'll go to the park and on Tuesdays, you'll visit the library.

Changing the poster and talking to your baby each morning about the plans for the day can benefit both maths and self-care development. Having a daily routine poster with simple pictures helps your baby learn time concepts such as "morning", "afternoon", "evening" and "before", "after", "later", and "earlier". If you update this poster as your baby grows, it will not only continue with teaching maths, it will also help avoid toddler meltdowns as you reassure your baby that snack time is not far away.

►ACTIVITY◄

Massage your baby

"Introduce baby massage sessions that make young babies feel nurtured and promote a sense of well-being."

(Excerpt from *Development Matters in the Early Years Foundation Stage Guidance* – Physical Development: Health and Self-Care p25)

As mentioned on DAY 40, massage can be a lovely way to teach babies maths through geometry positional language, sequences, and opportunities for counting fingers, toes, hands, legs, and strokes—all while also boosting their health and self-care.

* * * * * * *

Developing your baby's healthy self-care is important. So is developing his or her maths understanding. Luckily, you don't need to choose between them; introducing routines for these areas of development benefit both self-care and maths understanding.

DAY 53

Literacy

Reading

The *Early Years Foundation Stage Guidelines* for infants features only two suggestions for literacy. It is true that babies may not be independently reading or writing before they turn one, but an absolute wealth of information backs up the importance of reading to them, and introducing them to books as early and as often as possible.

At this age, the aim is simply to ensure your baby enjoys looking at books, hearing stories, holding books, seeing you enjoying reading—any of these provide an excellent foundation to literacy. When you read to your baby, emphasise the maths words included in the book and describe the pictures using maths-rich vocabulary. As noted in Professor Duncan's 2007 research paper 'School Readiness and Later Achievement', early maths was shown to be a more powerful predictor of later reading achievement than early reading of later maths achievement. Therefore, teach your baby maths and the literacy skills will naturally follow.

▶ ACTIVITY ◀

Share board books and cloth books

"Collect a range of board books, cloth books and stories to share with young babies."

(Excerpt from *Development Matters in the Early Years Foundation Stage Guidance* – Literacy: Reading p28)

Luckily, an abundance of number, counting, shape, and position books exist. However, do not worry if you would rather read a classic fairy tale or any other story; nearly all stories follow a set sequence with a beginning, a middle, and a happy ending. This introduction of sequences supports maths tuition.

Although this book focuses on improving numeracy, you'll find many recommendations throughout to introduce your baby to books. If you were to follow every suggestion made, of course your baby would have a great foundation in mathematics, but they would be well on the way to mastering key literacy skills as well.

Combine numeracy with literacy for a wonderful learning experience.

DAY 54

Understanding the World

As your baby looks around a room with interest and scans the environment for novel objects and events, he or she is becoming more aware of the world. And it just so happens that a baby's world is full of maths.

Babies realise this soon enough even without active teaching. But given their curiosity in everything from the curved sides of the spherical rattle to the probability of getting their favourite lolly colour from the pot, your input is still appreciated!

To make sense of a complex world, right from birth, your clever baby will use maths skills such as probability and classification. As previously mentioned, babies quickly categorise the adults around them into people they can trust and rely on for food and comfort versus those they should be wary of. Their learning relies on maths skills, so enabling those skills to grow will only expand their understanding.

Once again, you need not compromise when choosing between a focus on learning maths versus understanding the world. In fact, teaching your baby about the world using the language of maths not only helps him or her but might open *your* eyes to what you take for granted.

►ACTIVITY◄

Provide a soft play area

"Provide spaces that give young babies different views of their surroundings, such as a soft play area, with different levels to explore."

(Excerpt from *Development Matters in the Early Years Foundation Stage Guidance* – Understanding the World p39)

The more interactive and hands-on your maths teaching, the better. Let your baby pick the view and guide you toward what he or she is drawn to, whether it's the big cushion in front of your baby or the two toys behind him or her. "In front", "behind", "big", and "two" are all useful mathematical terms your baby will grasp faster than you might expect.

The world is full of maths.
Your baby is full of curiosity.
Embrace that curiosity and teach your baby maths.

DAY 55

Baby Curriculum Summary

The last few days have given you suggestions from the Early Years Foundation Stage Curriculum. These have demonstrated that your baby can follow the maths activities in this book and is, at the same time, following the curriculum and developing in all areas.

You may wonder what else the curriculum (free and available online) holds. But before you wade through the nearly one hundred suggestions for babies up to 11 months, it may be useful to know that more than 80% of the suggestions fall into these four, easy-to-implement categories:

1. Sing to your baby
2. Talk to your baby
3. Bond with your baby
4. Take turns with your baby

The benefits of each of these for teaching your baby maths are mentioned often throughout this book. How reassuring to know they also help develop all other areas.

►ACTIVITY◄

Sing 'My Hat It Has Three Corners'

It is perfectly possible to cover all four of the above categories with one fun song, as explained here.

1. Sing to your baby – A simple song such as 'My Hat It has Three Corners' has number and shape references to add to the maths experience.
2. Actively talk to your baby – Fold a paper hat, chatting as you do it. Point out the corners and count the number of points.
3. Bond with your baby – As you make the hat and chat to your baby, make eye contact. When singing to your baby, hold him or her close and enjoy the song together.
4. Take turns with your baby – Put the hat on your head and sing, "My hat it has three corners…", then say, "Your turn!" and put the hat on your baby's head. As you do that, sing "Your hat it has three corners…". Enjoy the back and forth patterns as you interact.

★ ★ ★ ★ ★ ★ ★

Sing. Talk. Bond. Take turns.
These simple actions will teach your baby
maths and much more!

DAY 56

Baby Curriculum Activities

Yesterday, you recognised that many of the activities in the curriculum fall into four distinct categories regardless of whether they were aimed at developing literacy, physical development, or maths. Today provides a chance to look at each of the categories in detail and do a few activities from the curriculum. You might be surprised how many you already intuitively do.

1. Sing to your Baby

"Say or sing made-up rhymes or songs while stroking or pointing to the babies' hands, feet or cheeks."

(Excerpt from *Development Matters in the Early Years Foundation Stage Guidance* – Personal, Social and Emotional Development: Self-confidence and self-awareness p10)

"Use finger play, rhymes and familiar songs to support young babies' enjoyment."

(Excerpt from *Development Matters in the Early Years Foundation Stage Guidance* –Literacy: Reading p28)

"Sing songs and rhymes during everyday routines."

(Excerpt from *Development Matters in the Early Years Foundation Stage Guidance* – Communication and Language: Listening and Attention p15)

These include just a few of the many singing-related suggestions drawn from across all areas of the syllabus. As you can see from the excerpt references, these three are taken from sections of the syllabus specifically aimed at developing personal, social and emotional development, literacy, and communication and language. It is impressive that, in so many areas of development, singing to your baby helps. Nursery rhymes are catchy and easy to remember, making them a great way to introduce new vocabulary for literacy and numeracy. Rhymes can be comforting and soothing, thus increasing your baby's feelings of secure attachment. Songs and music also encourage movement, sometimes via set actions but mostly from the natural enjoyment of the sound, rhythm, and beat. Most of all, they are a fun way to increase interaction and teach your baby maths.

Using rhymes to teach your baby maths will undoubtedly boost all other areas of his or her development.

2. Actively Talk to Your Baby

"Talk to babies about what you are doing and what is happening, so they will link words with actions, e.g. preparing lunch."

(Excerpt from *Development Matters in the Early Years Foundation Stage Guidance* – Communication and Language: Understanding p17)

"Use repeated sounds, and words and phrases so babies can begin to recognise particular sounds."

(Excerpt from *Development Matters in the Early Years Foundation Stage Guidance* – Communication and Language: Listening and Attention p15)

"Interpret and give meaning to the things young babies show interest in, e.g., when babies point to an object tell them what it is."

(Excerpt from *Development Matters in the Early Years Foundation Stage Guidance* – Communication and Language: Understanding p17)

These suggestions are about involving your baby in a conscious manner. Babies love the sound of your voice, but they learn most when they are engaged in the "conversation". This might involve talking about what is happening to them or focusing on what they are pointing at or interested in. A great way to increase understanding is to use gestures, pictures, or physical objects to emphasise key words. Remember, the more you talk, the more you can consciously incorporate maths words.

3. Bond with Your Baby

"Look at the baby and say their name. Make eye contact and wait for them to react."

(Excerpt from *Development Matters in the Early Years Foundation Stage Guidance* – Communication and Language: Understanding p17)

"Be close by and available, to ensure that babies feel safe and loved even when they are not the centre of adult attention."

(Excerpt from *Development Matters in the Early Years Foundation Stage Guidance* – Personal, Social and Emotional Development: Self-confidence and Self-awareness p10)

"Hold and handle babies, since sensitive touch helps to build security and attachment."

(Excerpt from *Development Matters in the Early Years Foundation Stage Guidance* – Personal, Social and Emotional Development: Making relationships p8)

For babies to confidently leave their primary carer and explore independently, they need to feel secure about returning and having their basic needs met. Any time you take to forge these vital bonds with your baby is not wasted. As a bonus, creating a secure attachment has been linked to increased intelligence test scores.

Babies are uniquely amazing in their ability to absorb new information and their desire to push themselves to develop. However, they need down time to process their new knowledge, to rest and just be loved. Listen to their cues and teach them what they want to learn when they want to learn it. That way, they will develop faster. No baby boot camp necessary. Just follow their lead.

Teaching your baby maths, or anything else for that matter, shouldn't be a forced, rigid process. Teaching your baby maths should be a natural, organic journey you enjoy together.

4. Take Turns with Your Baby

"Follow the baby's lead by repeating vocalisations, mirroring movements and showing the baby that you are 'listening' fully."

(Excerpt from *Development Matters in the Early Years Foundation Stage Guidance* – Personal, Social and Emotional Development: Making Relationships p8)

"Engage in playful interactions that encourage young babies to respond to, or mimic, adults."

(Excerpt from *Development Matters in the Early Years Foundation Stage Guidance* – Personal, Social and Emotional Development: Making Relationships p8)

"Play games, such as offering a small toy and taking it again to rattle, or sail through the air."

(Excerpt from *Development Matters in the Early Years Foundation Stage Guidance* – Physical Development: Moving and Handling p22)

These skills not only hone whatever action, facial expression, or noise your baby is practising and mimicking, they also teach social rules used in conversations and shared play. These are vital for later friendships and relationships as well as maths understanding. What's more, babies love the one-to-one attention they get playing turn-taking maths games like peek-a-boo or patty cake.

► A C T I V I T Y ◄

Sing 'Baa Baa Black Sheep'

'Baa Baa Black Sheep' introduces the numbers "one" and "three" and the maths concept of "full".

Before you start singing, find a suitable instrument such as a rattle, bell, or shaker. The first time you sing through the whole song, let your baby see you shaking the instrument, then pass it to your baby and say, "Your turn!" as you keep singing. This simple activity incorporates many key elements your baby needs to develop in all areas. As you sing and talk with your baby, you are bonding and tuning in. You are also introducing the idea of taking turns.

Do you see how you are boosting all areas of your baby's development as a result of teaching maths?

★ ★ ★ ★ ★ ★ ★

Singing, talking, bonding, and taking turns can be done separately, or you can combine them for even more fun!

MYTHS ABOUT MATHS

"As boys show greater confidence and willingness to learn math concepts at the start of school than girls, it seems likely that their early experiences with their parents are both gendered and influential."

– ALICIA CHANG,
Cognitive and Developmental Psychologist

DAY 57

The Maths Gene

Maths is amazing, beautiful, and useful, but it isn't always viewed in a positive light. Why? What puts people off maths before they even give it a chance?

Over the next few days, you will consider common maths myths. We start today with the idea that some people just don't have mathematical minds. You may have heard, or even said yourself, "I'm just not a maths person." Is there such a thing as a "maths gene"?

This is a dangerous myth—that some people just cannot do mathematics. Maths is simply a skill, like any other, that takes practice.

You may be thinking about children who seem naturally gifted in this area. They gravitate towards the number blocks and the logical Lego toys while others show little interest and seem to struggle with simple counting tasks. It can be tempting to write off those who appear less able.

According to research at the time of writing this book, no scientist has identified a maths gene. A small percentage of people (maybe as little as two percent of the population) have been diagnosed with dyscalculia. This makes it hard for them to manipulate numbers and often requires special teaching. However, as detailed on DAY 3, the evidence clearly states that introducing the language of maths early in life can positively affect a person's maths ability later in life. That's true for everyone!

However, parental expectations can certainly help or hinder maths progress. And on DAY 69, you will see how culture can play a role in defining a child's attitude to maths. In fact, in many cultures, the notion that there is a "math gene" does not exist; instead, people simply and sensibly assume that those who work harder know more.

For children who seem to naturally understand maths, you do not get to see all the mathematical experiences in their lives that shape their interest and ability in maths before they attend school. Outside of school, they have experiences with blocks, puzzles, toys, and games along with rich conversations with adults about maths concepts. Due to these experiences, some children appear to have a maths gene. This is actually great news! It means that your baby can be given the same head start.

It is incredibly important that, as a parent, you do not let your children doubt their numerical ability. If your child struggles with maths, it can be tempting to use the "maths gene" myth to convince yourself he or she does not have a maths ability. If children pick up on this myth, it can become a self-fulfilling prophecy. Most likely, they will give up and miss out on opportunities that having confidence in maths can provide.

►ACTIVITY◄

Positive reinforcement

By reading this book, you have already proven yourself to
be proactive and not someone who assumes maths ability
is predetermined at birth. Today's activity reinforces that,
regardless of genetics, your baby can do maths. On DAY 25,
you were introduced to positive affirmations confirming that
maths is good in general. The experience today specifically
affirms your baby is already good at maths.

Add these statements to your list of affirmations:

"The more we play, the easier understanding
maths is for you!"

"You get more confident with maths every day!"

"You can learn anything!"

**There is no maths gene.
"Maths is fun! You can do it!" Say this to
your baby often—until you and your baby
both believe it.**

DAY 58

Boys are Better Than Girls at Maths

This is a total myth. Both boys and girls can excel at maths.

An entire book can be, and no doubt has been, written about the impact of various gender-specific early influences. That includes the effect of media and the types of activities and toys parents introduce to their babies. For example, even storytelling can inadvertently reinforce gender differences, with boys being more likely to be told stories of autonomy and achievement while girls are more likely to be told stories about relationships and support.

Sadly, despite the abundant prose written about the necessity of gender equality, we still seem to live in a culture in which gender defines your baby.

Talking to babies about numbers has been shown to give them a maths skills boost, but why would this impact boys more than girls? Cognitive and Developmental Psychologists Alicia Chang and Catherine Sandhofer tracked the gender bias back to infancy. They studied the quantity of number words used by parents with their baby boys versus their baby girls.[21]

The results showed a clear difference in the way parents interacted with their baby boys compared with their baby girls. The researchers noted that parents draw boys' attention to numerical concepts far more often than they do for girls. Indeed, it turns out that parents spoke to their sons about number concepts *twice* as often as they did to their daughters. This difference in mathematical interactions is likely to affect their number skills later in life.

This study helps us understand how deeply ingrained gender bias is while emphasising how hard it is to give your daughter an equal start compared with boys in mathematics. The best (and only sure) way to ensure your daughter is numerically competent and has the confidence to succeed at maths is to introduce it plentifully in a fun way while she is a baby.

Take time to see if the words you use vary at all. How do you interact with each gender? Simple things like the toys children play with can influence the type and quantity of maths vocabulary used.

Picture helping your baby with building blocks. You may find yourself interacting with your baby boy using words such as, "Let's see how high we can build a tower! Can we make it bigger than the last one? That was four blocks high; let's try to make it five blocks high this time—the biggest ever!"

Using an identical pile of blocks, you may find yourself chatting to your baby girl saying, "Shall we start by using some of the blocks to make a nice bed for your doll to sleep in? We can get a blanket from the other play set to make sure she's really cosy."

In this example, with your son, you naturally use the rich maths vocabulary of "bigger", "four", "five", and "biggest". With your daughter, you only use the positional word "in" but the emphasis is not on maths.

Unfortunately, these are not extreme examples.

The ultimate goal? To live in a world in which all possibilities are open to your baby, where there are no gender differences and no limitations to your child's opportunities and choices. The perceived maths gender divide myth is highly damaging. It results in girls being far more likely to believe they cannot do maths or deciding early on they do not enjoy maths without having experienced its huge range of topics. This can have many undesirable consequences and may limit future options for females.

► ACTIVITY ◄

Compare how you talk to baby boys versus baby girls

Take time to look at the toys, books and activities you have available for your baby. Consider how these could influence the quantity and quality of your daily NUMBER TALK.

Pay attention as you hear other parents talk to their sons versus their daughters. But, be prepared to be shocked when you realise that Chang's finding of baby boys hearing double the number talk that baby girls hear may actually be underestimated.

★ ★ ★ ★ ★ ★ ★

**Your baby's gender does not define his or her maths potential.
It only affects *others' expectations* of his or her maths potential.**

DAY 59

Maths is About Worksheets and Rote Learning

It is easy to see why this maths myth might put you off introducing maths to your baby. It is true that some young children are expected to learn maths through repetition and rote learning. In the same way, it is true that some babies are taught to read using flashcards and memorising set words. However, neither of these enables the baby or toddler to fully understand and master the process. And flashcards rarely make the experience fun.

Some people assume the best mathematicians can instantly solve maths equations without errors. The truth is this: whether your two-year-old daughter is counting to three or your four-year-old son is learning how many sides a hexagon has, solving new problems or learning new material takes effort. By memorising and rote learning facts or repeatedly answering the same addition sums on worksheet after worksheet, your child could learn to get to the correct answer fast. But, it's more important to surround your baby with the language of maths in a fun, stimulating way. No worksheets are required for that!

Once babies understand the patterns, structure, and language of maths, everything else will fall into place. Ultimately, you want them to think and problem solve for themselves, not just memorise facts.

▶ A͟C͟T͟I͟V͟I͟T͟Y͟ ◀

Play with your baby

For today's focused activity, simply play with your baby.
Follow his or her lead. Do not start your play session with
an agenda. And *definitely* do not have a worksheet or flashcards to hand out. Just talk to your baby about his or her
immediate interest.

If your focused playtime happens to be tummy time on
the playmat, then notice how your baby leads you to talk
about geometry including shape and positional language.
Without planning or prepping, you will likely mention the
rattle **in front** or your baby rolling **over** and reaching for
the bell hanging **above**.

Learning maths is fun and instinctive—when you let it be.

★ ★ ★ ★ ★ ★ ★

**Aim for your baby to think and problem-solve
rather than merely memorise facts.
Let your baby's curiosity lead the way.**

DAY 60

It is Bad to Count on Your Fingers

Nothing is wrong with counting on fingers as an aid to doing arithmetic. In fact, counting on fingers indicates a fuller understanding of maths than if everything were memorised.

Stanford University's mathematics education research initiative, youcubed, finally dispelled the notion that finger-counting is only for children who struggle with maths.[22] Mathematics Education Professor Jo Boaler reviewed various studies from a branch of neuroscience that specialises in the part of the brain dedicated to the perception and representation of fingers, the somatosensory finger area. It seems that the visual cues and pathways in the brain are key to teaching and understanding maths.

If this maths myth persists and children are discouraged from counting with their fingers, it could slow their mathematical development. Do not forget that two of our brightest visual thinkers, Albert Einstein and Thomas Edison, were written off by teachers and even considered stupid.

Fingers are probably your most readily available and useful visual aid. They are also critical to mathematical understanding and brain development.

►ACTIVITY◄

Sing 'I Can Count'

I Can Count
(Hold up fingers as you count)

I can count, want to see?
Here are my fingers—one, two, three.
Four and five, this hand is done.
Now I'll count the other one.
Six, seven, eight and nine
Just one more, I'm doing fine.
The last little finger is number ten.
Now I'll count them all again.
One, two, three, four, five, six, seven, eight, nine, ten!

★ ★ ★ ★ ★ ★ ★

It is great to use your fingers to show
your baby how to count.
Make maths real and visible for your baby.

DAY 61

Maths is Not Creative

This myth rests on the fact that there is often a single right answer to a maths question. Because of this, maths can be seen as inherently deterministic rather than open and creative.

But what is creativity? The dictionary defines it as "the use of imagination or original ideas to create something." By this definition, mathematics must be considered a creative pursuit. After all, the mathematical world is governed by patterns—some known but others representing constant new discoveries.

You could say that once you get past the basics, then creativity is as central to mathematics as it is to art, literature, and music. In fact, maths can be found in all of these!

Maths becomes creative when you allow yourself to enjoy it and see what you can discover.

► ACTIVITY ◄

Make snowflakes for your baby to play with

This simple activity could become a family tradition that gets better and more enjoyable each year.

In real life, every single snowflake is unique, each one having perfect symmetry. Those facts alone inspire maths-related creativity.

To make a paper snowflake, fold a piece of paper a few times, and then cut out sections. When you unfold the paper, you will have a beautifully symmetrical, intricate pattern. If you make a few snowflakes, you can let them slowly float down on your baby. Be sure to watch your baby follow the snowflakes as they fall.

As your baby looks at each snowflake, talk about the symmetry.

★ ★ ★ ★ ★ ★ ★

Let your baby get creative with crafts or music.
Where fun and exploration happen, so does maths!

MUSIC AND MATHS

"Music is the pleasure the human mind

experiences from counting without

being aware that it is counting."

– GOTTFRIED LEIBNIZ,
17th century philosopher and polymath

DAY 62

The Importance of Music

Music is powerful. It can change a person's mood. It can unite individuals. It can build connections. Music also offers a joyful and rewarding learning experience that nurtures a baby's imagination, creativity, logic, rhythm, and understanding of sequences. It is powerful, indeed.

Like all the best teaching tools, music has the potential to engage multiple senses. For example, when you are rocking your baby while playing a song, you are stimulating his or her sound and touch receptors. This helps build strong neural pathways, and these pathways become even stronger through repetition. It is common to listen to a piece of music or a new song many times during a short space of time.

Why not have fun with varying the tempo of songs? For example, sing your baby 'Head, Shoulders, Knees, and Toes' and get progressively faster while still touching all the correct body parts. Use this opportunity to mention the maths words "quicker" and "slower".

As with all methods of teaching your baby maths, the learning process is designed to improve more than just your baby's maths skills. Music is no exception.

As your baby repeatedly hits the saucepan with a wooden spoon, bear in mind this noisy action is boosting his or her brain for learning and understanding maths. The brain seems to be wired in a way that links music and maths. What a super combination! It is even hypothesised that Mozart used mathematical concepts to create his musical masterpieces. Music and maths intertwine in ways that encourage both the left and the right sides of the brain to work together, combining the logical and creative parts.

So, encouraging your baby to continue pounding away at that "drum" is arguably a very good idea.

► ACTIVITY ◄

Enjoy music with your baby

Over the next few days, you will further explore the role music has to play in your baby's development. For today, take time to consider the role it plays in yours and your baby's routine. When do you listen to the radio? Do you play an instrument? Do you play familiar songs at bedtime? Do you go to concerts or other musical events with your baby? Did you attend such events before having a baby?

Listen to a baby song, lullaby, or nursery rhyme and see how your baby responds. If you are holding your baby, rock or sway in time to the music. Alternatively, let your baby move independently while on a playmat. Then put on one of your favourite songs and don't worry if it is pop, jazz, or classical. If you enjoy it, then your baby probably will.

You'll both find enjoying music is a magical, contagious way to have fun learning maths.

★ ★ ★ ★ ★ ★ ★

Let your baby explore the regular beat,
the measurement of time passing, and the
repeating patterns of music.
Absorb yourselves in music, and you will both be
immersing yourselves in maths.

DAY 63

Music and Social and Emotional Development

When babies learn to love music and associate it with a happy, carefree childhood, then their love of music will most likely last a lifetime. Music at any age is often a shared experience, be it rhyme time at six months old, choir at school, or dance lessons with their best friend. By its very nature, music is a social experience.

Along with the social side of music comes the emotional side. So much of social interaction comes down to managing and understanding your emotions and others, too. Music helps your baby learn and practise self-regulation. You already intuitively know this; you probably sing lullabies to soothe your baby. Maybe you dance while jigging your infant in time with an upbeat song as a distraction. Showing coping mechanisms like these to babies provides them with valuable tools to use as they grow up.

Music can also be used to help babies learn words to describe their emotions. For example, songs like 'If you're happy and you know it, clap your hands' are old standbys. You probably have favourites that evoke strong emotions. Sometimes, there need not even be words; just the feel of the song can make you bounce with joy or allow you the freedom to release negative emotions.

When it comes to your baby's social development, music seems to naturally draw people together. If you put out a box of bells, drums, and other musical toys, you may soon find your baby copying and joining in with other infants. In group baby music experiences, babies can rattle their own instruments whenever they choose and still be part of the ensemble. This allows a wonderfully natural bonding experience to occur while important social skills are being discreetly nurtured.

Music does, in fact, naturally encourage turn-taking, sharing, and patience. For example, some songs require an infant to follow a pattern and wait until a set part of the song before joining in, and others work best going around in a circle until it is your baby's turn in the sequence.

Learning happens most easily when the environment is right and your baby feels happy and secure.

▶ ACTIVITY ◀

Sing 'If You're Happy and You Know It, Clap Your Hands'

Use these as verse suggestions:

If you're happy and you know it, clap your hands...
If you're happy and you know it, stomp your feet...
If you're happy and you know it, shout hooray...
If you're happy and you know it, do all three...!

While this song is great for identifying emotions, notice the lovely repeating pattern to it. You see it even includes a number-related verse at the end. That's perfect for teaching your baby maths while having a lot of noisy, playful, energetic fun.

★ ★ ★ ★ ★ ★

Focus on the emotional and social aspects of shared music experiences, whilst the patterns and sequences present in music naturally teach your baby maths.

DAY 64

Music and Physical Development

It is almost impossible to listen to music and not move. A tapping of your foot, a drumming of your hand, or even a shimmying of your body. For most people, music is a whole-body experience. This is also true for your baby. Upbeat music time will most likely also be physical activity time. Even soothing lullabies can involve a rocking motion.

To help develop your baby's gross motor skills, simply hold and rock him or her as you move to the music yourself. In time, it will feel natural to hold your baby up while bouncing on his or her legs in a baby's interpretation of dancing. Any movement like this will build your baby's muscles in the arms, legs, and tummy.

Music activities also help babies develop their fine motor skills. So many tunes aimed at infants involve hand movements. Start by helping them form simple shapes like the mathematical diamond shape or the flashing stars in 'Twinkle, Twinkle Little Star'. Before you know it, your infant will be independently joining in with all the actions.

With games such as musical statues or by simply swaying to the beat, music can help develop balance. When babies are too little to stand, support their bodies and help them get used to the rocking, twisting motions that form a part of dance.

Music and movement offer a lot to your baby but why not go one step further and combine music, movement, and *maths?* Simply waltz round the room counting the one-, two-, three-beat rhythm out loud as you bob with your baby on the first beat.

► ACTIVITY ◄

Sing 'One Finger, One Thumb Keep Moving'

A key part of physical development involves your baby gaining an understanding of his or her body. It is hard to think of a more memorable way to learn about body parts than by singing 'One Finger, One Thumb Keep Moving'.

This song has lots of actions, a clear pattern, and repeated sequences. So, get moving! Enjoy the music, enjoy the movement, and enjoy the maths.

★ ★ ★ ★ ★ ★

Music is full of maths. Movement is full of maths. They partner beautifully for teaching your baby maths.

DAY 65

Music and Language Development

There's no doubt singing songs helps with language development. Songs support practising words and deciphering meanings, and they can be used to introduce a second language. Songs build phonemic awareness, which helps your baby hear, recognise, and form different sounds that gradually build into words.

Infants who can distinguish distinct sounds and phonemes are more likely to develop stronger literacy skills over time than those who don't. Music is a great way to support this because of the rhyming nature of songs and how some substitute one phoneme for another.

Hüseyin Serçe, a professor at Selçuk University carried out research[23] to ascertain if use of songs assists with recognition and retention of key vocabulary. Over a series of sessions, one group was taught specific words through popular songs while a control group was taught the same vocabulary through standard book-based tuition. The research findings confirmed that using popular songs was a more effective means to teach key vocabulary.

Given maths is full of specific vocabulary, and nursery rhymes include an abundance of key maths words, it is fair to say music promotes both general language skills and maths teaching.

►ACTIVITY◄

Make up a silly song

The language of maths is full of rich vocabulary. Have fun making up your own songs by picking a well-known tune and whatever maths words you would like to teach today. Include rhyming where you can.

Here's a simple one to sing if you're putting away the washing and want to introduce the mathematical vocabulary "odd" and "pair". Hold up the pairs of socks as you sing it.

The Sock Song by Emma L Smith (sung to the tune of 'London Bridge is Falling Down')

Let us put the socks in pairs,
Socks in pairs,
Socks in pairs.
Let us put the socks in pairs,
The odd one is over there!

You can make up silly songs anywhere, anytime. Some of your made-up ditties may even become family favourites!

* * * * * * *

Maths is full of new and interesting words for your baby to learn, and music aids vocabulary retention. Sing to your baby to teach him or her maths.

DAY 66

Music and Mathematics

While developing social, physical, and language abilities, it is clearly still possible to continue exploring maths with your baby through music.

Music provides an opportunity to practise patterns and thinking skills, improve memory, and reinforce numeracy knowledge such as shape names and other geometry language.

When it comes to learning number names and counting, you want to sing catchy, rhyming, repeating songs focused on this concept. For example, singing 'One, Two, Buckle My Shoe' helps reinforce any other number work you are doing.

A fundamental principle of maths is understanding patterns and sequences. Almost every song or piece of music has a pattern built into its melody or lyrics, so appreciating and anticipating patterns in music also reinforces a key maths skill. To support this, select songs with a repeating chorus or a surprise ending that your baby can anticipate after hearing them a few times. A good song for building anticipation is 'Pop Goes the Weasel'. Repetition and sequencing are apparent in 'Here We Go Round the Mulberry Bush'. And you can recognise a full story with a clear beginning, middle, and end in 'Mary Had a Little Lamb'.

When it comes to academic achievement, memory can be a powerful tool to help gain top marks in tests. Music assists memory.

(Everyone has experienced a tune that sticks in the mind even years later.) Thus, music can help your baby remember numbers, shapes, seasons, days of the week, and all sorts of other useful maths information.

Most tellingly, a correlation between children who play a musical instrument and their maths ability is well-known and generally accepted. While your baby may be too young to start piano lessons, embedding a love of music now will prove to be a valuable investment in his or her future.

Probably the most talked-about research into how music affects mathematical capability is the "Mozart Effect". This term comes from a 1993 study by Rauscher, Shaw, and Ky.[24] They found that students who listened to Mozart and then took a test of spatial reasoning performed better than those who listened to verbal relaxation instructions or silence.

This widely reported research resulted in a flood of commercial products claiming to enhance your baby's intelligence. However, the apparent increase in one area of mathematical skill was only a short-term boost, lasting about 15 minutes. That part of the study was never emphasised!

If parents want to help their children succeed academically, purchasing a CD they can listen to regularly is unlikely to do any harm. But the real problem occurs when parents substitute playing CDs for the hands-on collaboration that comes with playing and socialising with their children directly.

▶ ACTIVITY ◀

Play an instrument for your baby

If you play an instrument, play it for your baby often. Alternatively, take your baby to one of the many classical music concerts that specifically introduces babies to music.

When you read how beneficial music is for your baby's development, it can be tempting to quickly tick "music" off your to do list by playing a Mozart recording or leaving the radio on all day. But the easiest option is often not the most beneficial. If you want your baby to love music and benefit from what it offers, then being actively involved in his or her early music experiences is crucial.

As a parent, you want to make learning maths effortless for your baby. This book is about making maths fun and easy to fit in to everyday life. But it is *not* about finding instant, hands-off solutions. If you enjoy the process, your baby can enjoy the results.

★ ★ ★ ★ ★ ★ ★

**Look for the maths in music,
and you will find it.
Share that knowledge with your baby by
emphasising key words and patterns as you
sing, listen to music, or play an instrument.**

10

TOPICS OF IMPORTANCE

"Good numeracy is the best protection against unemployment, low wages, and poor health."

– ANDREAS SCHLEICHER, OECD

DAY 67

The Importance of the Pushchair

When you chose your pushchair, you probably considered how small it could fold and how easy it would be to push. Maybe even the colour or make was central to your selection. But did you choose it based on which type of pushchair would most help with your baby's maths confidence? Probably not.

As shown on DAY 2, the more you say number words to your baby, the better. With this in mind, it makes sense to consider how you can expand your dialogue—and especially your numerical chat—with your baby while he or she is in a pushchair.

Dr M. Suzanne Zeedyk, collaborating with the National Literacy Trust, showed that parents using a parent-facing pushchair spoke twice as much to their babies as those using the common forward-facing pushchair.[25] They also indicated that, in the parent-facing orientation, mothers and infants were both more likely to laugh.

Nature is full of mathematical concepts. Going on a walk allows you to talk about all sorts of maths-related topics. For example, you might say "Look at that **small** cat" or "I think that is the **tallest** tree" or "See **one, two, three, four, five** children in the park".

Amazingly, by simply changing the direction babies face in their buggies, we can easily double the number of words we say to them!

▶ ACTIVITY ◀

Play 'I Spy'

Play the game 'I Spy' when you are out for a stroll with your baby. If you chose "tree" you might start by saying, "I spy with my little eye…". As you say it, make sure a tree is in your baby's eyeline and add, "… something that is BIG!" Then use hand gestures to show if it is wide or tall. Make sure that, when you aren't looking at your baby, you are looking in an exaggerated way at the tree. Add an extra detail such as "… Something that is big and green…" If you see your baby look at a tree after your prompts, then say, "Yes! You are right. It's a big, green tree!"

★ ★ ★ ★ ★ ★

If changing the way the pushchair faces can double the number of interactions, what other small changes can you make to maximise your communication, engagement, and maths exploration with your baby?

DAY 68

The Importance of Screens

Plenty of DVDs and TV shows aim to teach babies about numbers. In fact, every year, parents spend hundreds of millions of pounds on them. But do they work?

It would seem not.

Dr Frederick Zimmerman led a study[26] in which he tracked how much time infants and toddlers spent viewing DVDs and television programmes. He found that for every hour a day that babies eight to 16 months watched educational programmes, they knew (on average) six to eight *fewer* words than babies who did not watch them.

If educational DVDs do not help, then what is the best way to teach your baby?

A different study[27] compared children who watched a best-selling infant-learning DVD several times a week with another group that did not watch the DVD. However, those parents tried to teach them the words from the DVD in their everyday interactions. It was found that the children who regularly watched the infant-learning DVD picked up few new words, regardless of whether they were watching alone or with a parent. In fact, they knew no more of the words from the DVD at the end of the study than children who had never seen it!

Unsurprisingly, the highest level of learning occurred in the no-DVD situation in which parents tried to teach their children the same target words during everyday activities.

What does this mean? As tempting as it is to use media to enhance your baby's learning, the best method has been shown, again, to be parental interaction on an everyday basis.

▶ ACTIVITY ◀

Teach your baby without a screen

Think about what you might hope a DVD or television show would teach your baby. If you have already invested in educational DVDs, watch them yourself to see what is presented. Then take the key words or concepts and introduce them to your baby yourself. Use this teaching moment to fully engage your baby's interest. Use all of his or her senses to get absorbed in the learning.

For example, if the programme presents simple shapes, primary colours, and favourite toys passing across the screen and choreographed around classical music, why not reproduce this yourself? You could play a Mozart piece in the background while introducing your baby to shapes. Instead of passively watching shapes pass across a screen, they can hold the shapes and feel the straight lines, sharp corners, or round curves. You would describe what they are seeing and feeling as they touch the shape. This makes their learning experience more real, personal, engaging, and memorable.

You are your little one's best teacher. Sing, play, talk, listen, and engage often. Then your baby can choose to delve into maths naturally at his or her own pace.

DAY 69

The Importance of Culture

Generalisations about gender and culture are just that—general-isations. However, when trying to better understand a complex topic, it can help to look at trends and averages. Where better to start than the much-reported triennial Programme for International Student Assessment (PISA) survey.[28] This grabbed headlines when the survey revealed that the highest performers came from Asian countries. In fact, in 2018 UK was a long way from the top slots and was positioned 18th in mathematics performance.

Why are children in the UK struggling with maths?

After these results were revealed, deliberation and theorising followed. Why doesn't the UK measure up with its Asian coun-terparts on the maths scale? Is our number system harder? Do we focus too much on literacy and not enough on mathematics in the early years? Is there too much play and not enough rote learning and worksheets in the UK education system? Many arguments have been put forward, most with some level of plausibility. However, a key recurring theme is related to expectations.

In the UK, our culture deems it acceptable for people to state they are no good at maths. Those who profess to enjoy mathematics are assumed to be "geeks" with limited social intelligence. With that stereotype, how can we hope the next generation will strive to fully embrace maths?

When setting and communicating your expectations, one simple truth is that your child can never choose to *drop* maths. Ability in maths is needed everywhere, in everyday decisions and processes. Even in seemingly non-numerical careers, children require some level of maths knowledge. And this requirement will only increase as society becomes ever more dependent on technology.

If you find yourself and/or others communicating their expectations to your child using sentences such as, "I was never any good at maths, and it didn't do me any harm"—watch out!

When reviewing approaches to infant development, it helps to compare which baby classes are available and how they're marketed. On DAY 39 to DAY 44 in this book, you saw that, while the UK has a large range of classes that benefits infants—all of which help teach your baby maths—none are marketed that way. There is no mention of maths in any of the class descriptions.

Compare this to a description of a baby class in Hong Kong: "… and provides more than just maths and science…" This highlights that maths education is *expected*; any other subject is extra. Another example: "Let your little ones absorb knowledge like a sponge. They use flashcards, pictures and dot cards to develop imaging, counting, and basic calculating abilities, while there are also activities to build upper body strength and balance." Again, the emphasis is on counting and maths skills, with other areas of development tagged on at the end of the description.

In the UK, maths is not a key focus for baby development—yet. Even invested, engaged parents tend to concentrate on literacy, music, and physical development. However, it has become clear there is an essential need to have a strong foundation in mathematics from as young an age as possible.

What would your friends say if you asked them, "What do you do to teach your baby maths?" Sadly, in the UK, parents rarely discuss how they're helping their baby maximise their maths abilities. Yet, having an open dialogue about maths in infancy helps set expectations while explicitly communicating the importance of maths to your baby. This provides excellent grounding for future learning.

Vast quantities of books about raising a literate, language-rich baby are available in the UK, but you'll find a notable absence of similar books for introducing maths. If, as a collective, we were confident enough to provide a strong foundation in maths for our babies, then they would respect maths as a worthy and necessary skill set.

Many areas of mathematics are objective in nature, often with clear right or wrong answers. So, unlike the more subjective disciplines, everyone starts with an equal opportunity to master the language and logic of maths, regardless of culture. The issue is not about competence; it's about confidence. Low expectations will undermine your baby's self-belief. That means if *you* believe maths is worth the challenge of mastering it, then *your baby* will too, and everyone will benefit.

▶ ACTIVITY ◀

Let your baby play with an abacus

The abacus is a calculating tool that likely dates back to 2700 BC. Used over the centuries, merchants, traders, and clerks in Asia still widely use it today.

Chinese education is known to be incredibly strict. In the early school years, students are often taught with an abacus until they no longer need it. Then they find themselves using an imaginary abacus that can be three times quicker than a calculator.

With its colourful beads like a fun toy, an abacus can reinforce maths concepts through touch. People might use it for counting, addition, subtraction, multiplication, division, square roots, and cube roots.

Today, you want to use it for counting. So, after moving all the beads to one side of the abacus, coax your baby to push any beads he or she chooses while you count the beads along the way.

★ ★ ★ ★ ★ ★ ★

Show your baby you think maths is
important and fun.
If you believe this and demonstrate it,
your baby will, too.

DAY 70

The Importance of Diet

Babies' brains develop more in the first year of life than at any other time. Therefore, it makes sense that the nutrients given to feed their bodies and brains during this period can affect their intelligence later in life.

In general, the key to achieving a nutritional boost in your baby's diet is to provide a variety of healthy foods—initially via milk and then by including a range of vitamins, minerals, proteins, carbohydrates, and good fats. Infants who are malnourished through this period may not adequately grow, either physically or mentally. Inadequate brain growth explains why children who do not have access to sufficient nutrients can suffer lasting behavioural and cognitive deficits. These might include slower language acquisition, delayed fine motor development, lower intelligence scores, and below-average school performance.

Research has shown a strong link between the following three nutrients and brain development.

1. Omega-3 Fatty Acids

A lot has appeared in the media in the past decade about omega-3 oils and their benefits. Over this period, a growing number of studies have linked the levels of omega-3 oils, especially DHA (docosahexaenoic acid found in omega-3 oils), with an infant's brain development.

Evidence from multiple studies points to the fact that increased DHA levels translate into better brain function.

2. Iodine

Research has found evidence that mild iodine deficiency during pregnancy leads to reduced intelligence in babies.[29] By age eight, babies born to mothers with low iodine had lower IQs by an average of three points compared to those born to mothers with healthy iodine levels.

3. Iron

Iron deficiency has also been linked to cognitive deficits in young children. Iron is critical for maintaining an adequate number of oxygen-carrying red blood cells, which in turn are necessary to fuel brain growth. Deficiencies in this mineral can adversely affect learning, memory, and attention span.

Diet will influence many health and intelligence factors throughout your child's life. It is worth putting time and effort into ensuring your baby starts eating a balanced, nutritional diet. This not only helps form good eating habits; it also boosts your baby's intelligence during a crucial phase of brain growth.

►ACTIVITY◄

Grow your own carrots

Seeing food grow and eating it fresh from the garden encourages children to eat more healthily. As well as your baby's brain developing due to all the wonderful nutrients, growing and eating your own carrots and other vegetables provides ways to teach maths during the process. For example, you would introduce the concept of time by looking at the difference in seasons for planting and harvesting. You would count down the number of days the carrots will take to grow. You would have a set time to water the plants. What other benefits come to mind?

★ ★ ★ ★ ★ ★ ★

Eating a healthy diet is important—for a healthy
body helps build a healthy mind.
More than that, in teaching your baby maths,
you can use food to understand addition,
subtraction, the concept of time, and more.
Diet really is important!

DAY 71

The Importance of Sleep

No new parent underestimates the importance of sleep. Something you may have taken for granted becomes the most precious of all commodities. Sleep is definitely vital, but is it important for maths ability?

In the womb, babies spend nearly 95 percent of their time asleep. For newborns, that may still remain as high as 18 hours each day. Sleep is important because your baby's body and brain are in a state of rapid development. While your baby sleeps, memories are stored, synapses formed, connections established, and energy replenished. Sleep is critical for brain development, especially in the first couple of years of your baby's life.

In fact, most of your baby's brain development happens during sleep. In addition, a lack of sleep can cause problems such as cognitive issues and developmental delays.

While asleep, babies' brains store what they learn in the day—and they have a lot of new information to process every day!

Psychologist Sabine Seehagen and team tested the importance of napping and its effect on a baby's memory.[30] In the study, six- and 12-month-old babies were taught a new skill, then half of them napped shortly afterwards while the other half stayed awake. The babies who napped remembered more of the new skill, both four hours later and 24 hours later. That indicates napping helps consolidate and cement the learning of new skills.

►ACTIVITY◄

Maths sleep routine

Today, incorporate massage or yoga into your baby's nap time and bedtime routines to aid sleep. Read a number book such as *My First Numbers Let's Get Counting* by Dawn Sirett and gently sing 'Twinkle, Twinkle Little Star' so your baby drifts off to sleep with thoughts full of numbers, shapes, snuggles, and happiness. While your baby contentedly naps, in effect you are fast-tracking his or her mathematical development. At the same time, you are earning some "you" time—or at least that's the theory. No harm in giving it a go!

★ ★ ★ ★ ★ ★

Sleep is key to developing your baby's brain— and any new skills learned before a nap are better retained. All the more reason to read a number book before putting your baby to bed!

DAY 72

The Importance of Baby Maths Toys

Most activities in this book are accessible for parents on all budgets. However, there is a place for educational toys to be purchased rather than made. Think about opportunities to stock up on them for birthdays and Christmas.

Toys need to be age appropriate. Anything too complex will not keep your baby's attention but neither will toys that are too simple. Also consider if a toy can be left out for your baby to pick up easily or if it requires adult supervision and playing with together. Both have their merits.

While some toys can be incredibly simple and cheap, others can seem excessively expensive. It is useful to consider the price per play and the toy's longevity. Don't write off expensive toys altogether. They may be played with for many years and in different ways as your baby grows up.

Experts have questioned needing expensive toys to boost a baby's IQ. There seems to be a trade-off between knowing that stimulation and novel experiences are good for brain development and understanding it does not all have to come from one toy. You can always introduce your baby to different colours, textures, and noises without buying expensive toys. Your baby does not need toys with expensive "bells and whistles" to learn. That said, if a certain toy is fun and gets *you* involved, it still has a benefit because your baby learns through *your* reactions.

When picking a toy, remember that, as well as learning from new experiences, your baby learns from exploring. If he or she happily plays by pushing a button or repeatedly knocking down towers, then find the patience to let that play continue. Do not let *your* boredom or your plan of what the play session should be pull your tot away from what seems basic to you. Allow your baby's brain to go deep into an activity, and the world he or she has created becomes a brain booster. Don't get stuck on too much of a schedule to miss that!

Let your baby solve any problem while playing with a toy, even if that means watching him or her struggle, get frustrated, and do it the hard way. Do not be tempted to save your baby the pain of experiencing failure; it's a great learning experience.

If you try to make your baby's life easier, then what happens? Over time, your baby will believe you do not think he or she can do it and will stop trying. After all, it's easier to automatically turn to you for help. But do you see the huge disservice this creates in the long run? Give your baby a chance to solve problems without correcting him or her. It's okay to do it the hard way. The satisfaction of achieving a goal independently will be worth all the frustration.

Before long, you will learn which toys stimulate your baby, and which ones gather dust. However, to get you started, a universally loved toy that promotes maths learning and will engage your baby for years to come is a set of building blocks.

Building blocks can range from simple cubes of wood to detailed plastic blocks moulded to fit neatly together. Using them with your baby, it is best to start with simple chunky blocks and let him or her see you do the building. But it won't be long until your baby is independently stacking, constructing, and learning with blocks. Your investment in building blocks will ultimately help with your baby's motor skills, hand-eye coordination, spatial reasoning, cognitive flexibility, language skills, creative and divergent thinking, social competence, and engineering skills. Impressive!

There is also evidence that block-play is linked with higher mathematical achievement. In one study,[31] the complexity of a child's LEGO play had long-term predictive power. Specifically, it showed that more complex play during early childhood correlated with higher mathematics achievement in high school—quite a benefit.

Another firm favourite is the activity cube. You will find activity cubes in most waiting rooms across the country—for good reason. This can be an ideal toy to let your baby explore easily and learn from over time. By leaving babies to work out which shape goes into which hole, they are recognising shapes, developing problem-solving skills, using their grip and the muscles in their hands and arms to manipulate objects, discovering concepts such as "in" and "out", and gaining a sense of confidence and accomplishment. By moving beads around a maze, babies develop fine motor skills, logic, and problem-solving ability. They also discover how things fall when they lift them up and how they can create a movement around the maze when they cannot take things out. They learn spatial awareness and gain an understanding of object permanence. When it comes to helping your baby's development, an activity cube is a toy worth investing in!

Other great toys to boost your baby's maths skills and general development include chunky puzzles, musical toys, stacking rings, shape sorters, tipping cups, and pop-up toys. To get the most out of a toy, let your baby explore it independently while you chat as he or she tries new things. Put names to the shapes your baby is slotting. Talk about the biggest ring being stacked first and say that you're impressed with your baby's determination to fit the shape through the hole.

►ACTIVITY◄

Do a jigsaw puzzle with your baby

You may think your baby is far too little to start doing jigsaw puzzles. But once babies can grasp things, they can hold a chunky puzzle piece and, with guidance, see how it fits into the space.

To do a jigsaw puzzle, your baby takes into consideration the shape of the pieces and where they belong as part of the whole. It also teaches the importance of thinking before acting as well as the link between logic and physical tasks.

Completing a jigsaw puzzle with your baby prompts you to use geometry language such as "in", "out", "left", "right", "turn", not to mention naming shapes and giving descriptions. It can also encourage you to use vocabulary linked to comparisons, patterns, and measuring. All of these strengthen your baby's understanding of maths in a fun, hands-on way.

★ ★ ★ ★ ★ ★ ★

**Let your baby explore and lead when playing with toys.
Let your baby learn from repetition.
Let your baby learn from failed attempts.**

DAY 73

The Importance of a Growth Mindset

The idea of instilling a growth mindset is not new. Professor Carol Dweck has been researching this topic for over a decade. As explained in her 2006 book *Mindset: The New Psychology of Success*, individuals can be placed on a continuum according to their implicit views of where ability comes from. Some who believe their success is based on innate ability are said to have a "fixed" theory of intelligence—that is, a fixed mindset. Others who believe their success is based on hard work, learning, training, and grit are said to have a "growth" or "incremental" theory of intelligence—that is, a growth mindset.

The importance of nurturing a growth mindset in your baby comes from realising people with a fixed mindset often shy away from new challenges. Why? Because they fear failure. Meanwhile, those with a growth mindset enjoy pushing themselves to try new things while learning from any failed attempts.

How do you help your baby approach new challenges with a growth mindset? Start with the following four suggestions.

1. Be a Good Role Model

As a new parent, you not only want to work on helping your baby have a growth mindset; you also want to work on your own attitude. Let your baby see you attempt new things and sometimes get it wrong. Children can view adults as infallible, so making errors in front of them demonstrates it is okay not to be perfect.

Unsurprisingly, a correlation exists between parents who see failure as a positive step and children who have a growth mindset.

2. Provide Novelty

Babies thrive when they're allowed to explore new toys and environments. They approach all new situations with limitless curiosity as an engaged and fearless new learner. To encourage your baby to follow his or her natural instincts and relish opportunities to acquire knowledge, constantly present new things and delight in the ups and downs together.

3. Make Your Praise Specific

When outlining NUMBER TALK earlier in this book, the K stood for "Keep Praising" and the advice was this: For every negative interaction with your baby, make sure you give at least five pieces of praise.

Although this is good advice, when considering a growth mindset, the advice needs to be more nuanced than that. Yes, give more praise than criticism, but don't be gushing about everything your baby does, especially if it is not praiseworthy. Dweck's research[32] identified that praising what the child did rather than the child himself or herself is a better type of praise.

For example, if you constantly tell babies they are clever, this promotes a fixed mindset. As they grow up, they might shy away from new experiences because they do not want to fail and shatter this belief. So rather than giving a generic "Good job!" or "You're so clever!" show them you have noticed their effort and praise their actions with a statement like, "I'm really proud that you tried different ways to reach your toys. Great problem solving!"

4. Celebrate Successes *and* Failures

Every time babies topple over, they are one step closer to sitting unsupported. Babies naturally push themselves. They do not stumble and then give up on learning to walk. Rather, they stumble hundreds of times and finally "get there". You will find yourself praising them every step of the way.

The same should be the case for learning maths. If your baby tries to fit the square in the triangle hole, take time to point out how close he or she came. You might say, "The triangle does have straight sides like a square, so have another go". When errors happen, respond with a smile and a "try again" message. This shows your baby the action was not a problem and to keep trying. Practise makes perfect.

It is important to let babies fail. If you take the shape and slot it in the right hole for them, you may stop them from being upset in the short term, but you will have deprived them of a valuable learning experience. In fact, you will have taught them you don't think they can manage it themselves.

Remember, there is a big difference between your baby enjoying a challenge or struggling with a task. If you assume he or she is struggling, you want to jump in at the first whimper and help. Don't do it! This will reduce any confidence in achieving the task without assistance. If you see your baby reaching for a toy on the playmat, see it as one more challenge to learn from. This might not feel easy, and your baby could get frustrated. But after achieving the goal, he or she will feel immensely proud—even more so after you give your praise.

►ACTIVITY◄

Maths Motivational Mantra

Keep this motivational mantra in your mind as you watch your baby striving to achieve:

I never fail.
I either succeed
or learn.

Today, let your baby play with a shape sorter toy or a homemade slotting toy and watch him or her rise to the challenge. Your baby may not manage it today, but it's a learning experience every time the shape does not fit. That's especially true when you give verbal guidance and positive reinforcement.

★ ★ ★ ★ ★ ★ ★

Encourage your baby to explore and grow while praising the effort, not the result. Celebrate both success *and* failure.
These simple actions will give your baby the gift of a growth mindset.

DAY 74

The Importance of Maths Exams

Would you rather not revisit your school day maths lessons? If so, you're not alone.

You have probably realised that teaching your baby can be different. No classroom, no right or wrong answers, no tests or assessments. Just fun and a chance to bond with your baby. But now might be a good time to revisit this key question: *Is maths really the right area to focus on?*

You may have heard of the knowledge gap in terms of literacy and the importance of reading to your baby as much as possible. No doubt this is important, but if you had to choose one area to focus on, the evidence shows that maths is even more influential than reading.

You now know the level of maths children have achieved *before* school may indicate their later academic success. But why are later academic achievements and school qualifications important? In particular, why do you need maths qualifications?

General Certificate of Secondary Education exams or GCSEs are a stepping stone to further qualifications and future careers. Your baby will enter school before you know it. Your child will spend the following decade preparing for GCSEs. These exam results will be the markers used to judge your child's ability across a range of areas and subjects.

Mathematics is deemed such an important GCSE that pupils are required to re-sit the exam if they fail it the first time. You may know your child is intelligent but without qualifications to prove it, many doors will be closed. GCSEs, especially mathematics, can prove to be an important door opener!

The negatives associated with no qualifications are clear, but what are the benefits of pursuing a mathematical route in further education?

Having even a basic mathematics qualification demonstrates your child can think logically and process information to determine solutions to a wide range of problems. These skills will impress future employers and enable your child to embark on earning a degree in the science, technology, engineering, and mathematics (STEM) field.

Maybe you're not sure your child will want to pursue a career in such a technical environment. In that case, consider the variety of career paths under the STEM umbrella. Possibilities include the design of video games, sound engineering for the music industry, developing new cutting-edge sports equipment, designing lifesaving medical equipment, creating new recipes, inventing technologies to reduce carbon emissions. The list is impressively diverse.

A significant number of UK businesses rely on people with STEM skills. To meet current demand, the number of people with STEM degrees already needs to increase. Forecasts indicate that this number will only rise in the future.

Future employment prospects look promising if this is the path your child chooses. These STEM roles are well remunerated, with maths graduates often earning more than graduates of other areas.

In summary, if you can instil a love of maths in your baby and he or she goes on to achieve maths qualifications of GCSE level or beyond, then you enable your child to have access to a wide range of opportunities.

►ACTIVITY◄

Read The Pythagorean Theorem for Babies

Dealing with GCSEs and A Levels probably feels a long way off and not relevant to how you spend your time with your baby today. Thinking about topics such as Pythagoras theorem, probability, and calculus might not seem suitable for your baby. However, Mike Ziniti, a mathematician and actuary, has written a series of maths for babies' books, under the pseudonym Fred Carlson. Titles are:

* *The Pythagorean Theorem for Babies*
* *Non-Euclidean Geometry for Babies*

The Pythagorean Theorem for Babies introduces three shapes: a square, a rectangle, and a triangle. Nice and simple. It continues to highlight the key concepts required to understand Pythagoras theorem using bold diagrams and simple explanations—definitely worth sharing with your baby.

★ ★ ★ ★ ★ ★ ★

Maths qualifications can prove to be advantageous door openers!

DAY 75

The Importance of Maths for Adults

For adults, maths and general numeracy are needed constantly for everyday tasks: paying for shopping, telling the time, reading time-tables, getting the best price—the list is endless.

Understanding maths is important beyond achieving at school. It may surprise you that one in five adults have a numeracy level lower than that expected of a nine-year-old.[33]

As a parent, it is only natural you want the best for your children even when they are adults. While money does not guarantee happiness, a lack of it can make life more challenging. Intuitively, it seems a link would exist between maths ability and earnings. The Skills for Life survey[33] conducted by the DfES confirmed this with a finding that those workers with GCSE level maths or above earned £8,000 more on average than those with a lower numeracy level. The survey also found the correlation between earnings and numeracy was stronger than between earnings and literacy.

Looking beyond financial security, when parents are asked what they hope the future holds for their children, they often respond that main goals are being healthy and happy. A basic maths understanding can assist with achieving this goal. One study shows that, among 34-year-olds, those with functional numeracy were half as likely to report having symptoms of depression than those with poor numeracy.[34]

Finally, most parents would love their children to grow up to be independent. Jon Carpentieri's research paper 'Adult numeracy: a review of research'[35] identified that men with poor basic numeracy skills have almost twice the likelihood of remaining in their family home well into adulthood rather than moving out and enjoying independence. When considering females, women with poor numeracy skills had double the likelihood of experiencing homelessness, with one out of ten women suffering this fate.

Teaching your baby maths can be a fun way to engage and bond with your baby. More important, it can lay the foundations for your little one to approach future maths learning with confidence. This could have far-reaching effects throughout life.

►ACTIVITY◄

Play supermarkets

Today, talk to your baby when you get money from the cash machine, pay for coffee, and count your change. While you cannot let babies play unsupervised with coins, you can let them know what coins are used for. Toddlers love playing "shops" and so can your baby. For example, as your baby reaches for the plastic banana, you can say, "Would you like to buy one banana?" As your baby looks at you and coos, continue the conversation using maths-rich vocabulary associated with money.

Some specific maths vocabulary used in the curriculum includes: left over, money, coin, penny, pence, pound, price, cost, buy, sell, spend, spent, pay, change, dear, cheap, costs more, costs less, costs the same as, how much does it cost?

Use terms like these during shopping playtime and when you use money in your everyday activities.

**Maths is important—to your baby now and to the adult he or she becomes.
Everyone needs maths every day.**

11

FORMING A MATHS HABIT

"Good habits formed at youth make

all the difference."

– ARISTOTLE

DAY 76

Forming a Maths Habit Overview

You have been teaching your baby maths for 75 days, and you know from the preceding days that:

1. Babies seem to be born with an amazing number sense: understanding shapes in the womb, being aware of quantities at seven hours old, assessing probability at six months old, and comprehending addition and subtraction at nine months old.
2. The best time to introduce maths is infancy. By the time children enter school, there is already a significant gap in maths skills.
3. A parent's attitude shapes a child's attitude. You have the power to teach your baby that maths is enjoyable and not something to be anxious about.
4. Your baby can learn maths while boosting all other areas of development. For example, movement will be boosted while teaching geometry positional language, literacy will be boosted while reading a "number" book, and bonding will be boosted while giving your baby your undivided attention teaching maths to him or her.
5. Babies will use maths every day for the rest of their lives. That's why maths is important.

You know the theory, and you have been doing maths activities with your baby for the last few months. How can you make sure this becomes something you keep doing, even after finishing this book? By embedding these activities into your routine. With minimal effort, you will have given your baby an enormous gift with lifelong benefits.

Also review why you are teaching your baby maths. Is it because you have anxiety around maths, and you do not want your child to feel the same? Is it because you believe maths will be important for future careers and independence? Is it because you think understanding maths can improve all areas of your baby's development? What will keep you reading, singing, and talking to your baby after you have finished working your way through this book? It's important to understand your motivation to begin building a maths habit.

Whoever wants to build a habit must believe the time invested will be worth it. If not, the habit will be viewed as hard to form, and maths will become a chore (or not happen at all).

Give yourself time to create a new habit; some say it takes 21 days. In the 1950s, Maxwell Maltz, a plastic surgeon, noticed that his patients took a minimum of 21 days to adjust to the results of their surgery. He also observed that, for patients who had an arm or a leg amputated, they would sense a phantom limb for about 21 days before mentally accepting their new situation.

Maltz wrote a highly acclaimed best-selling book called *Psycho-Cybernetics* that had a significant influence in the self-help professional community. Unfortunately, the "21 days" term became established in people's memories, while Maltz had said "*a minimum* of 21 days."

While 21 days creates a simple timeframe to work toward—short enough so you feel forming a new habit is possible but long enough to be believable—it has been based on casual observations, not scientific facts. So, what do scientific studies indicate about forming habits?

Dr Phillippa Lally, a health psychology researcher at University College London, studied how long it can take to form a habit.[36] Her study examined the habits of adult volunteers over a 12-week period. At the end of the 12 weeks, the researchers found that, on average, it took *more than two months* (60+ days) before a new behaviour became automatic.

Also, how long it takes a new habit to form can vary widely depending on the behaviour, the person, and the circumstances. In Dr Lally's study, it took anywhere from 18 days to 254 days for people to fully embed a new habit, although it should become easier and easier the more days you stick to it.

Interestingly, the researchers also found that messing up once or twice did not affect the overall habit formation process. That indicates building better habits is not an all-or-nothing process. Just keep doing your best.

What does this mean to you with regards to embedding the habit of maths? It means you keep working your way through the activities and invest time in the process. You'll find some habits form quickly and easily while others take more effort. However, if you allocate an amount of time almost every day—and persevere for 60 days—then you will have given yourself and your baby a good chance of establishing life-changing, lifelong maths habits!

►ACTIVITY◄

Set a calendar reminder

Pick one maths habit—maybe a bedtime number book—and choose a specific time to do it each day. Set a calendar reminder for every day to read a story at that time.

★ ★ ★ ★ ★ ★ ★

It's wonderful to give your baby the gift of 100 days of maths activities; but building a maths *habit* is a gift for life.

DAY 77

Forming More Maths Habits

If you believe it is good to have one maths habit, such as reading your baby a book each day, then having two or three or more must be even better!

It is helpful to anchor a habit to something you already do, such as nappy change or bath time. Then, as you include more maths habits each day, they can be anchored to each other. For example, once you have established the habit of reading to your baby each night, it is not a huge leap to add a 30-second sleepy song. The next step might be to add a short massage as you change his or her nappy and put on night clothes. The mathematical words in the book and song followed by the sequences your baby will learn from the massage will be a great way to end the day.

The more you get into a routine and anchor habits to different parts of the routine, the easier and more intuitive it will be to remember to do them.

►ACTIVITY◄

Add a lullaby to story time

When your calendar reminder pops up today for reading a bedtime story, add a lullaby such as 'Twinkle, Twinkle Little Star.' Let your baby drift to sleep with geometry filled thoughts of **little diamond** and **star** shapes **up in** the sky.

★ ★ ★ ★ ★ ★ ★

If one maths habit is good, then two or three or more must be even better!

DAY 78

Dealing with the Obstacles

What gets in the way of forming a maths habit for you?

It can be tempting to flick through a book like this and be inspired to introduce as many maths activities as possible. If you have been persuaded of its importance and understand there is no time to lose, then you may want to cram in as much "teaching" as possible. This is great. However, it may not be sustainable. Babies take a lot of time and energy to care for. Introducing even one new element into their routine requires effort and careful planning. Give yourself space to decide which maths activities might become everyday events and prioritise those when you are building your maths habits.

The ideas in this book may sound wonderful in principle, but the reality of starting a lifelong maths habit might still seem alien to you.

When babies are little, it can be hard to see the positive impact of these maths activities. For example, when you show them how to count their peas and they just throw them all on the floor, "now" may not feel like the time to form maths habits. If you feel disheartened, then keep doing the daily activities and, just for a short period, don't think too much about why you are doing them. Instead, think of the maths activities as daily experiments.

If you or your baby dislikes one day's activity, then stop and do a different one the next day. But if you both enjoy it, do not worry if you cannot see immediate maths benefit. Every suggestion is designed to teach your baby maths, but the activities also help with literacy, social engagement, physical development, bonding, and more. If you are not convinced you want to specifically teach your baby maths, then regard the activities as a simple way to bond with your baby. If you accidentally teach your baby maths in the process, so much the better. And if your baby falls happily asleep after a relaxing massage and a few nursery rhymes, then the experiment is surely worth continuing.

Yes, it is easier to build a habit if you believe in it. But regardless, it is important to build these maths habits *now*. You may not immediately see the benefits, but it will all be worth it when you finally do.

Do you have a common obstacle or a perceived difficulty you keep coming up against? For example, "I don't have enough money to buy number books" when there are free books at the library or "my voice isn't very good for singing nursery rhymes" when your baby couldn't care less how "in tune" you are. These can be excuses to stop rather than genuine issues that are hard to overcome.

If you did not enjoy maths as a child, you might identify lots of obstacles. In that case, it is even more important to help your baby enjoy the maths activities so that he or she does not develop the same fear. Don't give up entirely on any action because of a minor hurdle.

You can overcome obstacles by working through them with friends, family, or other new parents. To embed daily maths habits, you can encourage each other. For example, if you have a weekly coffee morning with friends, bring your baby's favourite book and share story time. This will encourage other parents to give it a go, too. Talk about how your baby responded to the pop music you played or the mirror you gave them. Show them how they can wriggle their fingers as you sing 'Twinkle, Twinkle Little Star'. If you share this book with others and agree to work through the activities together, you will feel motivated to keep going.

It can be seen as "geeky" to enjoy maths. It can be seen to be "helicopter parenting" to engage with your baby. Do not let name tags put you off. Let people know you are teaching your baby maths—and you're both loving it!

►ACTIVITY◄

Play with Play-Doh

Today's activity is playing with Play-Doh.

What is your first thought as you read that statement? Are you enthused by the idea? Or are you thinking you do not have any pots of Play-Doh in the house? Or do you believe you won't have time today but maybe on the next rainy day?

You can overcome the first obstacle by making your own version of Play-Doh. Depending on what you have in your cupboards, choose from the abundance of easy recipes available online.

If time is an issue, is there another activity you have enjoyed before and could squeeze in? Maybe today is best suited to talking to your baby as you get on with your tasks. If so, the "Name What You See" activity on DAY 5 might be a good choice.

Know that it's possible to do a maths activity each day. First, though, identify what is putting you off. See if you can find an alternative that will help you build this habit one way or another.

* * * * * * *

Have you encountered any obstacles on your baby's maths journey? Don't worry; just keep doing your best!

12

MATHS HABIT 1 - TALKING

"Speak to your children as if they are the wisest, kindest, most beautiful and magical humans on earth, for what they believe is what they will become."

– BROOKE HAMPTON, author

DAY 79

The Habit of Talking

If there was only one thing you took from this book, it would hopefully be the importance of talking to your baby.

When talking to babies, the subject does not matter; the more you talk, the more they will learn—about everything. It is as simple as that. Yes, a few numbers thrown in along the way will certainly benefit them, but as you get into the habit of talking, you will find this happens naturally.

Maths is everywhere, in everything we do. If you are chatting about day-to-day things, then the maths language will be flowing without you even knowing. When you think about it, many simple sentences like these have maths vocabulary included:

"Let's put **on** your shoes, **one**, **two**."

"Look at that **little** doggy."

"You've already drunk **half** your milk!"

"I'm just going to lift **up** your legs to put your new nappy **on**."

As with other maths habits such as reading, treasure basket, maths corner, and five-minute focus (to be discussed), in addition to teaching your baby maths, the focus is now on forming the underlying habit.

As mentioned, the first step of forming a habit is to believe in it. Therefore, it makes sense to revisit why talking to your baby is incredibly valuable.

Your baby will learn a lot just from the environment—seeing, smelling, hearing, feeling, and tasting new things. However, detailed studies have shown that talking to your baby in the first three years of life is especially vital when building the brain architecture that's needed later to support reading, maths, and thinking skills. Specifically, research by Betty Hart and Todd R. Risley in *The Early Catastrophe – The 30 Million Word Gap by Age 3*[37] showed that children from talkative families may have heard 30 million more words directed to them by age three than children from less-talkative families. Hart and Risley linked the fact that the more words the children had heard by age three, the better they did on tests of cognitive development.

Their study showed this early advantage did not lessen as the children went to school, instead the knowledge gained in those formative years remains as building blocks for all future development.

Lots of affectionate talk from loving adults also builds healthy relationships and social skills for your baby. It is the one-to-one nature of talking that matters. Your baby cannot learn language (or much else) from a television set or background noise. Rather, the brain lights up with face-to-face interactions, and social connection opens it to learning.

The next question is this: Why is talking so important for maths knowledge?

As mentioned earlier, the maths-related language expected from five-year-olds when starting school includes more than 500 words. There is the issue of different words meaning the same things (for example, one add one, one plus one, one and one, the sum of one and one, the list goes on). Add to this an entirely new set of symbols (for example, +, -, =, >, etc.) that your child will need to understand and be able to manipulate. With those facts in mind, it becomes clear how important learning the language of maths is.

It is common for children entering school to understand how to count on one more from a number but not understand that is identical to adding one. Or they can happily share four sweets with a friend but have no idea this is the same as four divided by two. This results in maths being not only a set of rules to learn but a complicated, multi-faceted language to explain these rules. Often, a child can understand the concepts in practice but be thrown by the vocabulary.

This is where the talking habit comes into its own. The more you talk, the less of a mystery the language becomes. From the moment your baby wakes up, get into the habit of giving a running commentary on your baby's environment, activities, and what you are doing. This occurs as you change a nappy, at the supermarket, in the car, outside pushing the buggy. Tell your baby what he or she is looking at, what the surrounding sounds are, where you are going, etc.

Remember to give your undivided attention as you sing and read to your baby. Follow your baby's gaze to engage about things that interest him or her at that point in time. The more your baby is engaged in conversation, the more he or she will benefit.

What's the best way to fully involve babies? Let them choose the topic based on what they are looking at, pointing at, or doing at that time. Nouns are a great place to start—body parts, animals, toys—to introduce key words in a simple way. The maths teaching comes from describing these nouns through questions as you ask and answer, "How many are there, how big are they, what shape are they?"

Talking can happen anywhere and at any time; you just need to get into the habit.

▶ ᴀᴄᴛɪᴠɪᴛʏ ◀

Have a playdate

Babies find their peers more relatable than the adults around them. They can listen to the rhythm, pitch, and volume of other babies' vocalisations. Do not worry if they just blow raspberries at each other! This is an important developmental stage in language acquisition. Babies blow raspberries as they begin to understand their lips can come together to make sounds. Cooing and bubble blowing are also common in the early months. By nine months old, your baby will start to understand and express tone. Soon after that comes his or her first true words.

Let babies engage with each other but take the time to help by adding comments such as "There are **two** balls. Would you each like to have **one**?"

Talking to your baby feeds his or her curiosity and provides words to better understand the world. Much of what is explored through your communication contains maths.
Follow your little one's lead, and the NUMBER TALK will naturally do the teaching.

DAY 80

Long Sentences

As touched upon in DAY 79, introducing key basic nouns is a good way to get in to the talking habit. However, a study by Dr Anne Fernald,[38] a Stanford University psychology professor, found that using long sentences can be especially beneficial.

For example, you might say, "This is an orange." But it has been shown to be even better to give more context and say, "Look at this big orange in the fruit bowl next to the red apple." Study results suggest that the 30-million-word language gap cannot be breached by just hearing lists of words. What really makes a difference is hearing rich, varied language with good grammar that trains babies' brains to learn through context.

This idea of using long sentences fits well with teaching your baby maths. For example, when describing most nouns, the use of shape- and size-related terms can only help with both extending your sentences and introducing your baby to maths.

The following list includes key "shape" and "size" words found in the curriculum for five-year-olds: shape, pattern, flat, curved, straight, round, hollow, solid, corner, face, side, edge, end, cube, pyramid, sphere, cone, circle, triangle, square, rectangle, star, size, bigger, larger, smaller, and symmetrical.

Use maths vocabulary as often as possible to extend your sentences and teach your baby maths.

►ACTIVITY◄

Make your sentences longer

Incorporate maths words into sentences to make them longer and more stimulating for your baby. Here are two examples:

Short sentence: "There is your ball."

Long sentence: "There is your red, **spherical** ball. It is **next to** your **big** doll."

Short sentence: "You have cheese for snack."

Long sentence: "I have chopped your cheese into **three small cubes** for your snack."

★ ★ ★ ★ ★ ★

Simply increasing your sentence length as you talk helps you include lots of maths-rich descriptive words about shape and size.

DAY 81

Parentese

The *quantity* of words heard by your baby is undeniably important; however, it has been shown by researchers that the *quality* of words heard is also key. In addition to the importance of one-to-one communication and social context, success in language is also linked to the use of "parentese" or infant-directed speech.

If you have always lived slightly in fear of becoming one of the cooing, gooing, gaaing adults who talk nonsense to their babies, fear not. Nobody is suggesting you go down that route. Parentese is using a sing-song voice with extended vowels made up of no nonsense words with slightly exaggerated pronunciation. Parentese is not baby talk, so you would not be using sounds like, "buba wan ikle nana." Instead, it uses correct grammar but extra vowel emphasis like this: "Hellooo baaaaby, dooo youuu want a baaanaaanaaa?"

Parentese is slower than normal talk. Each vowel and word become distinct, which makes words easy for your baby to discern. The pitch is higher than normal, which matches the limited range of your baby's vocal tract.

You can use this form of baby talk when going about everyday activities such as saying, "Where are your shoooes?" and "Oh, this tastes goooood!" You are emphasising important words and speaking slowly, using an upbeat, fun tone of voice.

The results of a study[39] led by Nairán Ramírez-Esparza and Patricia Kuhl found that babies who heard more one-on-one parentese leaped ahead of the others in language development. Around age one, they babbled more than babies who heard less one-on-one parentese. When the babies turned two, parents checked off a list of 680 words based on the MacArthur-Bates Communicative Development Inventory Words and Gestures checklist to report how many words their children knew. Babies who had heard the most one-on-one parentese had a more extensive vocabulary than those who had heard the least: 433 words vs. 168 words.

If this way of speaking does not come naturally to you or you feel silly, try it for five minutes a day in the privacy of your own home. As with building any habit, you will find it worth the effort.

►ACTIVITY◄

Sing 'The Grand Old Duke of York'

Sing 'The Grand Old Duke of York' to introduce your baby to the maths vocabulary of "up" and "down" using parentese.

Slow down the tempo and articulate clearly with elongated vowel sounds for the key maths words "uuuup" and "doooown". Sing it through once, lifting and lowering your baby as you emphasise the maths vocabulary. Then say the following words starting with your baby's name. (Research suggests that by three months old, babies turn their heads when their names are called and then focus on the next word.)

"Yes (baby's name), uuuup. He marched them uuuup to the top of the hill."

"Then (baby's name), doooown. He marched them doooown again."

Try this: When you are speaking, raise the pitch of your voice by as much as an octave and exaggerate your eye contact, raised eyebrows, big smiles, and other facial expressions.

The *quantity* of words you say to your baby is undeniably important. But the *quality* of words is key, too.
Use parentese to boost your baby's maths vocabulary.

13

MATHS HABIT 2 - READING

"Children are made readers on the

laps of their parents."

— EMILIE BUCHWALD, author

DAY 82

The Importance of Books

It is not possible to over emphasise the importance of books. For many reasons, you should start reading to your baby as soon as possible. Regular sharing of stories improves your baby's literacy, vocabulary, empathy, self-control, understanding of right and wrong, relationships, social bonds, listening skills, and imagination. Reading can also increase parent-child communication. And that is before considering the maths-related reasons: books give a lovely introduction to numbers, counting, and shapes. They raise IQ, increase attention span, introduce causality, and teach about sequences and logic.

What a persuasive list!

Many studies provide evidence of the benefits of reading, but one that's particularly interesting was carried out by Professor Manuel Jimenez.[40] It is a common phenomenon to see parents using a screen (phone or tablet) to placate their baby and keep them quiet (for example, when they're out at a restaurant). However, this study showed that, in fact, infants are less likely to be disruptive or hyperactive when they are read to regularly. So, by reading to your baby and forming a positive habit, you may not need to resort to screens to pacify your baby.

The study also found that parents who read to their infants were less likely to exhibit harsh behaviour toward their children. It noted that regular reading provides both emotional and academic benefits that can help increase a child's success in school and beyond.

It is interesting how often putting in a little more effort initially can reduce issues later. Starting a reading habit with your baby is a tried-and-tested example of this.

►ACTIVITY◄

Discover new baby maths books

1. Baby Einstein – My First Library 12-Book Set

This 12-book set includes important maths areas such as seasons, shapes, movement, and counting.

2. The Puppet Company – Traditional Story Sets: Goldilocks and the Three Bears

This set includes the three bears and Goldilocks puppets and makes counting three bears visible and real for your baby.

3. Counting Kisses: A Kiss & Read Book

This book brings together social bonding and counting into one lovely board book.

As mentioned before, *any* book will teach your baby maths, so do not delay starting to build a reading habit with your baby.

Don't delay; start a reading habit today!

DAY 83

Books and Teaching Your Baby Maths

These five benefits of reading emphasise the importance of books in your baby's maths education.

1. Provides a Fun Introduction to Numbers

A vast range of fantastic number books are specifically aimed at babies: board books, touchy-feely books, books with noises, books with mirrors, plus many more. When introducing your baby to numbers, reading a book each day will help. Do not worry if the book is not a number book, you'll find that most baby books have an element of maths teaching, whether that be counting, shapes, opposites, measuring, or sequencing.

2. Raises IQ

Reading to children in an interactive style raises their IQ by over six points. This was the finding of a study titled 'How to Make a Young Child Smarter: Evidence from the Database of Raising Intelligence'. [41] Within this study, using an "interactive" style of reading refers specifically to a technique known as dialogic reading. This involves engaging a child actively in the reading process via use of questions. Until your baby can talk and lead the storytelling, preparation for this form of interactive reading involves asking questions that don't require a verbal response—for example, "Where is the ball?"

Increased IQ will help your baby in all areas of academic achievement, including maths. However, this study also identified no increase in intelligence associated with reading interactively with a child over four years of age. Again, this indicates, when teaching your baby maths, the earlier the better.

3. Increases Attention Span

In the first few weeks of your child's life, you may feel silly showing him or her pictures when your baby is looking in the opposite direction. But persevere. A two-minute cloth book shared with your newborn baby will become a five-minute board book chewed by your six-month-old and then will develop into a ten-minute shared story with your one-year-old. You will feel amazed the first time your baby turns the page and delighted the first time you are asked for more. Ultimately, you will feel so proud the first time you see him or her "reading" a book alone.

Reading regularly helps babies enjoy books and appreciate the reward they get for concentrating until the end of the story. Any structured learning requires focus and a developed attention span, and none more so than maths.

4. Introduces the Concept of Causality

An important element of maths is the concept of cause and effect—that actions have consequences. Books are a great tool for teaching your baby this idea and will enable them to apply this learning to more abstract scenarios.

5. Shows Sequences and Logic

Nearly all books have a clear structure: a beginning, a middle, and an end. While interacting with your baby as he or she starts to understand stories, you can encourage critical thinking and the application of logic.

Enjoy reading with your baby—the warm snuggles, the bonding, the quiet time absorbed in the pictures, and more. Enjoy learning new concepts and language. But mostly enjoy knowing that whichever book you choose will help deepen your baby's understanding of maths.

▶ ACTIVITY ◀

Bring a book to life

Any book will teach your baby maths, but you can add an element of interest to bring the book to life. For example, if you read your little one a 'number' book with images of one ball and two apples, then have one ball and two apples at hand that they can hold. These real, visible items will help your baby better understand both the book *and* the maths numbers. Keep your sessions short but regular and, most of all, have fun.

How many times can you fit in a quick story time with your baby today?

★ ★ ★ ★ ★ ★ ★

Reading to your baby provides a fun introduction to numbers, geometry, measuring, and so much more.
Are you convinced yet of the need to get reading to teach your baby maths?

DAY 84

The Habit of Reading

Books are good. Reading is good. Hearing stories is good.

The first step to making something a habit is to *believe* in it. A lot of money has been invested in highlighting the importance of you reading to your baby because it's a key area to help development.

Sharing stories will not only improve your baby's literacy, but, as outlined on DAY 83, it will also teach your baby maths. Investing time to make reading a habit for your baby has been shown to increase the chance he or she will grow up to love reading. This is an amazing gift! The gift of never being bored. The gift of imagination. The gift of knowledge.

Let's look at five ways to start a habit that lasts a lifetime.

1. Schedule Time

Time is a funny thing when you have a new baby. Sometimes a short period seems to last forever; other times, a day disappears and you don't know what you achieved. Some parents naturally fall into a routine, so adding a slot for story time is relatively simple. If you are less schedule-focused, though, you may need to have tactics "at the ready" to ensure your baby gets exposed to books as often as possible.

The key is to keep your commitment and initial expectations low. We have all had those moments of deciding to, for example, give up sugar entirely, lose half our body weight, or learn a new language in five days. Rarely are such huge goals attainable or maintainable. Similarly, if you are not in the habit of reading with your baby, then start with the goal of sharing one short picture book a day.

By linking books to your bedtime routine, you are forming a positive habit that could last a lifetime. Reading stories at night gives your baby quiet, wind-down time and a cue that it will soon be sleepy time.

As children start reading for themselves, it is far easier to fit in their phonics and reading homework every night if you already have an established reading slot in their schedule. As they grow to be independent readers, it can be a lovely way to end the day, especially if you have another child who needs your attention. Allowing children to read in bed for half an hour before lights out may end up helping them—and you—finish the day in a calm, positive way for years to come. Definitely a habit worth forming.

Ideally, reading should fit into your day as often as possible. If the bedtime rush does not work for you, try to find some alternatives. You could invest in plastic bath books or ones that attach to the pram to enjoy outdoors. With so many opportunities to enjoy a story throughout the day, find ones that best suit you and allow reading to become a habit.

2. Always Have a Book with You

Always carry a book. This is great advice for anyone of any age but particularly good if you have a baby or a young child who needs to be distracted. If you are stuck in a doctor's waiting room, having a book will help pass the time. If you are meeting your friend and baby in a café and they are running late, this is an ideal time for five minutes of storytelling distraction. If you get into the habit of having a book in your bag, in the change bag, attached to the pushchair, in your car (you get the idea), your first instinct will be to reach for a book several times a day.

The reading habit will not only benefit your baby but help *you* get through any awkward, unscheduled waiting times, too.

3. Go to Your Local Library

Libraries are amazing places. They make it possible to borrow and read books for free. They often have free weekly story time sessions.

Inevitably, regular library visits lead to more stories and more exposure to a vast variety of books. Any of them can teach your baby maths, even if a book has no numbers, shapes, prepositions, patterns or story sequence. Simply pointing out page numbers and saying you are reading the first, second, third page will help your baby keep learning. When your baby begins to toddle, simply let him or her explore and choose books that seem interesting.

Some libraries have huge, oversized books that you would be loath to buy and store at home, but they add an element of fun to the proceedings. Libraries might have storytelling bags with puppets and props to bring the story to life. The props keep babies riveted by firing up their imaginations and love for stories. They also provide a real, visible way to show babies **three** bears or **five** ducks, for example.

Do not be put off by the thought that your baby would never keep quiet in a library. Libraries welcome all ages and librarians understand the need for a little bit of noise. All in all, taking a trip to your local library is a great routine to get into.

4. Visit Nearly New Sales and Bookshops

Yes, you have access to free books via your local library, but it feels special to own a few books and have them available to read again and again.

The variety of books available for children of all ages is staggering. And when you go to a nearly new sale or charity shop, you will see how inexpensive children's books can be. You can even utilise the purchasing opportunity to reinforce the maths area of money with your baby.

Several large book shops offer café facilities in a welcoming environment. Why not have a special outing to a book shop and make purchasing a brand-new book a big event? This fun treat can become linked to the joy of stories, reading, books and learning maths.

Certainly, any positive exposure to books helps build the reading and maths habits for your baby.

5. Make It a Treat

"Settle down with a hot chocolate on a big, soft cushion and listen to an enchanting story. When the story is over, we will have an art and craft session to recreate the characters from the book and make our story come to life!"

This is an excerpt from a local pre-school's club list. Wow! Four-year-olds wouldn't want to resist this!

Sharing a story and watching the sequence of events unfold should not be forced or rushed or seem mandatory. It should not feel like a chore or an obligation. Rather, it should feel like a magical, fantastic treat for you and your baby. For babies, achieving this is simple because their biggest treat is to have your undivided attention.

You can always enhance the moment with comfy cushions, a warm blanket, a cosy hug, a favourite cuddly toy, and the knowledge of it being a special time together. No phones. No distractions. Just the story and the special moment.

▶ACTIVITY◀

Set up a pretend library

Trips to the library greatly add to your weekly routine, but if your local library is closed or you do not have time, recreate aspects of a library outing in your own home.

Gather a pile of books and chat as you put them into categories: size of book, topic, board books, paperbacks, etc. Whatever categories you opt for, keep them simple and easy to describe. As you pick up each book, show it to your baby and ask if he or she thinks it is **big** enough to go in the **big** book pile or if it is **smaller** than those books.

Of course, stop and read one of those books when your baby shows an interest!

★ ★ ★ ★ ★ ★ ★

Responding to your baby's needs requires you to form many habits—feeding, dressing, napping routines, etc. But your baby won't automatically realise the joy of reading books. It's up to you to make reading a habit!

DAY 85

Top Five Barriers to Reading

Reading with your baby is good, and the benefits are clear. So why doesn't every parent do it? There is no one answer to that question. If this is a maths habit you believe in and want to form, then be aware of potential hurdles so they do not trip you up before you get started.

1. Cost

Books cost money. With a new baby, spare money can be a scarce resource. Do not let this put you off, though. It is possible to gain access to free books by borrowing them from the library, from friends, as birthday gifts, and so on.

Do not forget that, while your baby may love the pictures and visual aspects of books, a made-up story is free. Your made-up story can provide many of the lovely elements you would get from reading a book and you can tailor it to include whatever maths vocabulary you choose each night.

2. My Baby Might Damage the Book

It can be incredibly frustrating when your baby views a book as a fun thing to rip and break. If this puts you off launching a reading adventure, then start your baby with plastic, cloth, or board books. With their bright colours and interesting textures, these books are designed specifically for early introductions—ideal for your hands-on baby!

3. No Spare Time

Being a parent is a busy, demanding job; no one doubts that. To find time to squeeze in reading with your baby, you must believe in its importance. It does not have to be the same person who reads every time. Feel free to share the responsibility—as well as the snuggles and fun—with others who help care for your baby. Also get creative and read a story while, for example, bathing your baby, during feeding time, at nappy change. It does *not* have to be a large time commitment. Any story time is better than none.

4. I'm Not Good at Reading Stories

It has been discussed in this book that a parent's attitude of not liking maths influences their child, the same is true about reading. For the sake of your baby's development, you need to demonstrate a love of books and reading. Why? Because your baby will copy you and learn from you.

Do not worry. You do not need to be a master at doing silly voices or making up enchanting tales. You just need to engage with your baby, read the words, point at the pictures, and make it a warm, fun time—for both of you.

5. My Baby Is Not Interested

Initially, babies have a short "alert" time between feeding and napping. To ensure reading stories is a positive experience, picking a good time is important.

Learn to read babies' signals. Looking away from the book does not necessarily mean they are not enjoying the interaction. If they don't seem to be following the story, they are probably still absorbing a lot more than you realise. However, if they cry or become agitated, just leave it awhile and try later. The alert, active time increases quickly as they grow. Just give it time.

Don't let these barriers prevent you from forming a reading habit that will benefit your baby for the rest of his or her life.

►ACTIVITY◄

Make a book

The activity of making your own book immediately removes two of the barriers stated above: the book is free, and it does not matter if it gets ripped.

It can be as simple as folding a few sheets of white paper in half and drawing on each side. You could do bright two-dimensional shapes such as a circle, a triangle, a rectangle, a square, and a diamond. You could make a numbers book and draw the corresponding number of dots, or flowers, or cars on each page. Or you could make a sequences book and, on each page, draw a picture of your baby's daily routine.

Books and maths make a wonderful combination.

★ ★ ★ ★ ★ ★ ★

Anything worth doing does not come easy. Yes, you may face barriers to creating a reading habit but persevere—it will be worth it.

14

MATHS HABIT 3 -
TREASURE BASKET

"You will never change your life until you change something you do daily. The secret of your success is found in your daily routine."

– JOHN C. MAXWELL, author

DAY 86

The Treasure Basket Habit

In some ways, this is the hardest but possibly most rewarding maths habit to form. The hard part comes from the time commitment to regularly update the contents in the treasure basket. The reward is the excitement you will witness each time your baby discovers a new activity inside—well worth the extra effort!

The idea behind a treasure basket is that each evening, you put a different activity in a special place. This need not actually be a basket; it could be a toy cupboard, an old cardboard box, a gap under a desk, a corner of the room with a blanket over it—you get the idea. A treasure basket's most important aspect is its excitement—its air of mystery—as your baby opens it each morning.

If you use a box for the treasure chest, you might introduce the activity by twisting the box around while saying, "Round and round the box it goes, what is inside? Nobody knows. . ." followed by the big reveal! You want to make the build-up fun and exciting to get your baby fully engaged, ready for the entertaining, rewarding activity time.

If you can maintain the discipline of restocking the treasure basket, then as your baby begins to explore as a toddler, he or she will go with interest to see what mysterious activity has arrived overnight. Initially, you will need to be highly involved in the process, but as time passes, you will find that a few minutes of preparation can buy you pockets of time while your baby is entertained.

There is an increasingly common concern that children can have an abundance of toys and still feel "bored". It can be hard for them to choose a toy and get stuck into playing independently. In some cases, their lives are overscheduled, and downtime is far too rare. This treasure basket habit helps steer your baby towards an activity that cuts out the indecision associated with choosing from too many toys.

When babies are still little, the activities in the treasure basket need to be parent-led and interactive. However, as they grow, you can include toys they have forgotten about such as colouring sheets, stickers, picture books, dressing up clothes, a jigsaw puzzle, magnetic letters, Play-Doh—the list is endless.

Restocking the basket to engage your baby does not need to be a time-intensive process. A little thought can provide fun opportunities for your baby's maths development.

►ACTIVITY◄

Introduce your baby to a new treasure basket

Take a moment to decide where you want to store each day's activity. If it is a box, then decorate it together with your baby. If it is a cupboard, then clear it out and get it ready as you talk to your baby.

Pick one of your baby's favourite toys and do a test run of this new activity for the next day. You might introduce a sand timer at the first big reveal. Sand timers visually demonstrate the passing of time and can be mesmerising to babies.

This activity is certain to help teach your baby the maths concept of time.

★ ★ ★ ★ ★ ★ ★

Having a daily treasure basket activity takes effort. But give it a go, and you'll find the preparation time is worth the excitement and maths boost you create for your baby each day.

DAY 87

Treasure Basket Activity: Scarves

Swish. Twist. Float. Twirl. Bounce. Wave. Scrunch. Toss. Peek-a-boo. Up high, float down. Fast or slow. Round and round. Side to side. Over your shoulder. Behind your back. Through your legs.

Scarves are a fantastic sensory prop to use with your baby. They also take mere seconds to pop into the treasure basket. Experiment and find many fun ways to play with scarves, each of them helping your baby develop.

For example, you can play peek-a-boo by draping a scarf over your face and then pulling it off to reveal that you never disappeared. It works well to sing a song or talk gently to your baby as you do it, communicating that you are still there. In time, your baby will most likely put the scarf over his or her head and do peek-a-boo unprompted. Peek-a-boo is a fantastic way to introduce fun sequences.

You can also use scarves to waft over your baby. This will feel soothing or tickly, depending on your baby's mood. Try a few different textured materials—soft, woolly, rough—and let your baby feel the different sensations.

Scarves can also be waved from one side of your baby's face to the other. This helps with directional tracking as your baby's eyes follow the scarves' movement while giving you opportunities to introduce maths words such as "left" and "right".

In terms of introducing the language of maths, any movement of the scarf can help your baby to understand positional language, including prepositions, e.g., the scarf is moving up, down, in, out, over, through, or around.

To help babies improve their hand-eye coordination when they are older, throw a balled-up scarf in the air and let them catch it. It works well because a scarf floats more slowly and is easier to grab than a traditional ball. You can float the scarf at different speeds based on various tempos of music or use the scarf as a superhero's cape as you tell an adventure story. The options are endless. Each one will enhance your baby's development and increase the bond with you.

▶ ΛCTIVITY ◀

Scarf memory and counting game

Put three scarves, three small cuddly toys, two balls, and a
rattle in the treasure box. When you open the box, reveal
all the items to your baby, then hide the cuddly toys under
one scarf, the balls under another scarf, and the rattle under
the third scarf. If your baby can crawl, then let him or her
explore each scarf and, together, count the items revealed.
If need be, you can whisk a scarf off yourself to reveal which
toys are underneath. For safety reasons, be careful not to
leave your baby alone with the scarves.

As your baby approaches 12 months old, he or she will
understand sentences such as "Where are the two balls?"
and "Under which scarf are they?" This creates a lot of fun
for both of you!

★ ★ ★ ★ ★ ★ ★

Scarves are wonderfully versatile, and it only
takes a moment to put one in your baby's daily
treasure basket.

DAY 88

Treasure Basket Activity: Mirror

This is a super-simple, convenient, and inexpensive activity. Just pop a mirror in the treasure basket, and you'll have hours of cognitive-enhancing fun.

Even newborn babies are drawn to people's faces—definitely Mummy's face but also their own faces (not that they will know it as theirs yet). Have fun with these activities:

1. Use the mirror to pull funny faces and see if your baby imitates you. Anticipate plenty of giggles as "the baby in the mirror" also pulls faces.
2. Help your baby learn new words by pointing to his or her nose, mouth, and one, two eyes in the mirror.
3. Play peek-a-boo by pulling away the mirror and seeing how your baby responds.

A classic psychological experiment performed with babies and mirrors relates to babies' self-awareness. In a test conducted in the 1970s, researchers took a group of children aged six to 24 months and put a red dot on their noses. They let the infants see themselves in the mirror and discovered that those under 12 months old seemed to think the baby in the mirror was another baby. They happily interacted with this new baby, smiling and approaching the baby in a friendly way.

At 13 to 20 months as the babies became toddlers, they tended to be more hesitant in their response. However, it is not entirely clear they were aware they were actually looking at themselves in the mirror. By 20 to 24 months, though, the more mature toddlers seemed to fully recognise the reflection in the mirror as their own. The clear indicator was that, while looking in the mirror, they touched the red dot on their own nose instead of touching the face in the mirror.

Give this test a go yourself with your own baby!

►ACTIVITY◄

Tummy time mirror game

When you let babies play on their tummies, place a mirror in front of them so they can look at themselves as they play. Use maths movement words to describe where the mirror is. Then move the mirror to one side and the other. Where is the mirror? **In front**, **behind**, **beside**, **above,** to the **left,** to the **right**?

Babies love looking at themselves in the mirror, so most will probably twist around, roll over, or crawl towards the mirror.

The vocabulary to use should include key maths words such as over, under, above, below, in front, behind, beside, next to, opposite, left or right.

★ ★ ★ ★ ★ ★

A mirror is one simple item that facilitates many activities. It's the perfect treasure basket toy.

DAY 89

Treasure Basket Activity: Instruments

Music is great for your baby's physical, emotional, intellectual, and social development. It can improve listening skills and concentration; it helps relax or energise him or her; it can help increase vocabulary and, of course, maths skills. In short, music is good for your baby.

Using the treasure basket is a simple way to introduce your baby to music. If you belong to a local toy library, it might be possible to borrow a drum, tambourine, or maracas and then pop them in the basket for your baby to discover the next morning.

But do not worry if you don't have an instrument at hand. You can have fun making one at home. You could either assemble the instrument the night before or put the components into the treasure basket and do it in the daytime when your baby can "help".

Here are possible homemade instruments:

1. Shaker: At its simplest, this is an old plastic bottle with buttons, pebbles, dried pasta, or similar objects inside. You can have fun decorating the bottle with stickers, paint, and even ribbon.
2. Cymbals: Clang together two saucepan lids—if your ears can bear it!
3. Xylophone: Fill several glasses with different levels of water

and add food colouring to each to make a beautiful rainbow water xylophone. Tap on each one with a spoon to show your baby how the note changes depending on the water level in each glass.

4. Matchbox Guitar: Stretch elastic bands around a matchbox and twang away.

These instruments are fun, simple, and quick to prepare—if a little noisy!

▶ ACTIVITY ◀

Make an instrument

Put a saucepan and a wooden spoon in the treasure basket.
As your baby hits the "drum" with the spoon, count the
beats together. Music and maths so often go hand in hand.
So, it's hard to know if babies enjoy the music and that
inadvertently boosts the maths learning, or if they are drawn
to the sequences and patterns of maths and that leads them
into making music!

★ ★ ★ ★ ★ ★ ★

**Music and maths make a wonderful partnership!
Celebrate this by putting an instrument in the
treasure box for a noisy and fun activity.**

DAY 90

Treasure Basket Activity: Sensory Items

Learning happens best when all your baby's senses are engaged. This occurs constantly in a natural way as your baby explores and investigates the surroundings. But what if you create specific sensory experiences as you plan and explain what your baby is feeling, seeing, and hearing? Doing this can pave the way for future development.

Using your treasure basket, plan a sensory encounter that will entertain and help your baby develop by trying these ideas:

1. Light Show: Pop a torch in the basket and use it to make shadow animals, help your baby track the beam across the wall or ceiling, and wow your baby by flashing the light. Count the number of flashes or talk about how the **circle** of light gets **bigger** as you move the torch further from the wall. Mesmerising maths!

2. Play-Doh: Narrate your actions as you split a **sphere** of Play-Doh in **half**. Then sit back and watch your baby squidge, squeeze, and squash the dough. As your baby grows into a toddler, you can include a laminated sheet with shapes, numbers, or patterns to replicate in Play-Doh. You can revisit this experience many times in many ways. Malleable maths!

3. Textures: Include different bits of material—soft, rough, silky, stiff—to let your baby feel different textures. Gently brush them against your baby's skin or let them grab and hold items. As your baby crawls, you can set out a texture area and let him or her move across bristly mats, silky scarves, spongy play mats, etc. Which textures does your baby enjoy most? **How many** different textures can they feel? Are the bumps **big** or **small**? There are so many maths questions you can ask and answer as your baby explores. Memorable maths!

4. Water: This readily available, wonderful substance is completely non-toxic and easy to wipe up off a kitchen or bathroom floor. You can have hours of fun tipping and splashing water with your baby. The pot of water is **full**, splash! Now it is **empty**! Messy maths!

►ACTIVITY◄

Bubble play

Babies of all ages love bubbles—watching bubbles, popping bubbles, catching bubbles. Count the bubbles in the air as you blow them. Notice their spherical shapes and comment as they slowly drift downward.

Sensory play can make maths mesmerising, malleable, memorable, messy, and so much more.

★ ★ ★ ★ ★ ★ ★

You can always rely on sensory play to make exploring maths memorable. Embrace this when you choose any of the many sensory items readily available around your house.

DAY 91

Treasure Basket Activity: Books

Books are a recurring theme when it comes to giving your baby the best start on his or her maths journey. Hopefully, you are already well underway with the "reading to your baby" habit. Including a book in the treasure basket is a great way to ensure your baby chooses to have a story.

When time is at a premium, pick any book—an old classic or a new, exciting book—to grab your baby's attention. Put it in the treasure basket. When your baby discovers it, sit back and enjoy the moment, all the while knowing you are boosting your baby's intelligence in wonderful ways.

►ACTIVITY◄

Put a book in the treasure basket

A book such as *Ten Little Caterpillars* by Bill Martin is a perfect way to combine reading and an engaging maths activity. This beautifully illustrated book introduces various different caterpillars for your baby to find on each day. The caterpillars transform into butterflies allowing you the opportunity to talk about and point out patterns and symmetry. The book not only shows a clear set of maths number symbols from 1 to 10 but also goes through the sequence of ordinal maths words—first, second, third through to tenth.

Include in the treasure box the book plus ten wiggly caterpillars, which could be pieces of string or decorated lollypop sticks. Be as imaginative and creative as you wish. You can use this activity to count, discuss sequences, and consider symmetrical patterns.

★ ★ ★ ★ ★ ★ ★

Books are a wonderful way to teach your baby maths. But you already know this!

DAY 92

Treasure Basket Activity: Slotting Boxes

Your baby will love to slot things! You might find bits of food in the DVD player, toys down the back of the radiator, or even pebbles filling your shoes. While this child-initiated slotting can be frustrating and more than a little messy (even slightly destructive), it serves an important developmental purpose. Slotting helps babies develop their fine and gross motor skills and fires up their curiosity and imagination as they assess size and shape.

Making your own slotting machine is incredibly simple. Use an old box and cut appropriate size and shape holes to match the items you have available to be slotted. Alternatively, simply use a plastic bottle. Let your baby slot items that fit through the neck of the bottle, no cutting required.

Which items could you slot? Plastic shapes, dried pasta, and pebbles work well. But any toy could be used as long as the hole for slotting matches its size and shape.

►ACTIVITY◄

Make a slotting box with your baby

Talk while you make the slotting box. Discuss the different size holes using maths vocabulary such as, "bigger" and "biggest" to describe them. Count how many holes you are cutting out. Then let your baby choose an item from a box of differently shaped bits you have collected from around the house or on a walk. Be sure to cut a hole big enough to fit the chosen object. Make the whole process highly interactive.

Also, take this opportunity to introduce lots of mathematical language. For example, you might say, "That car is too **big** to go **in** that hole" and "Turn the plastic triangle **around**".

Your baby loves to slot, and slotting teaches the maths areas of shapes and measurement. What more could you ask for from a treasure basket activity!

DAY 93

Treasure Basket Activity: Sorting Games

Sorting or classification happens almost immediately for newborn babies. They have to assess who to rely on for food and protection. They know impressively quickly who their prime carers are, identified by smell and sound as much as looks.

It is not surprising the innate and essential maths skill of sorting motivates them to sort other things, just for fun. This nurtures their desire to make sense of the world.

By sorting, babies understand that things can be the same or different. Getting practice with sorting at an early age is important for learning additional mathematical concepts in due course. Logical thinking starts them on the path of making order out of a confusing world.

To get started with sorting, initially introduce two categories at a time (e.g., red pom poms and blue pom poms) while keeping other aspects of the selected item the same to avoid confusion. As your baby grows, you can add categories and make the differences less distinct.

Start by helping your baby take items from the treasure basket and sort them into different piles. Alternatively, you can use sorting trays, bowls, cups, egg cartons, divided containers, or paper lunch bags. Or you can simply line up the items or stack them.

As you carry out the sorting process, talk to your baby about the objects' differences and similarities. You can purposefully make an exaggerated mistake and watch your baby take a long look at the item in the wrong pile. This indicates a recognition that having a red item in the blue pile (or vice versa) is surprising to your baby. He or she knows it isn't right!

► ACTIVITY ◄

Play the sorting tidy-up game

Play the tidy-up game with your baby "helping" or at least watching. Explain what you're doing as you, for example, put all the dinosaurs in one box and all the cars in another.

★ ★ ★ ★ ★ ★ ★

Watch your baby go from sorting to comparing and classifying in no time!
Encourage doing this fundamental maths skill as often as possible.

DAY 94

Treasure Basket Activity: Stacking Toys

It is simple to put a few blocks or stacking cups into the treasure basket, knowing these toys can provide both fun and development opportunities.

In the first few months, stacking is too advanced, but young babies still benefit from watching you do it! As you enjoy this activity together, use plenty of mathematical language.

"Let's put the **biggest** block at the bottom."

"Next, we'll put the red **cube on top**."

"Look, this tower is **taller** than that tower."

"The blocks are going to fall **down** soon."

Before long, your baby will anticipate the stack toppling and get great pleasure from it.

As babies learn to sit and crawl, they love being in control of knocking the tower down and, towards the end of their first year, will probably attempt to build their own tower. At this point, they are developing their fine motor skills, not only to pick up the blocks but also to release them at the appropriate point. They need to use their pincer grip for small items, and their hand-eye coordination will certainly be important.

Your baby will be strengthening his or her brain by engaging the cognitive skills necessary to assess the problem and try different approaches. It will take concentration to experiment with various solutions, but all of these are excellent skills to prepare your baby for future real-life mathematical scenarios.

►ACTIVITY◄

Plastic cup games

Today, use one treasure basket item—plastic cups—for these activities:

- Stacking: Help your baby build and destroy a plastic cup tower. Include turn-taking with you building the tower and your baby knocking it down.
- Nesting: Putting cups together reinforces maths vocabulary with such words as smaller, bigger, smallest, biggest, etc.
- Skittles: Line up the plastic cups and let your baby see you roll a ball at them, knocking them over. Alternatively, let your baby be the ball, crawling forward and bashing the skittles over. Ask and answer such questions as, "If there were ten skittles, how many are left standing? How many were knocked down?"

Keep the number talk flowing throughout the mayhem!

★ ★ ★ ★ ★ ★ ★

Stacking toys provide an engaging activity for your baby to enjoy time and again.

15

MATHS HABIT 4 - MATHS CORNER

"There should be no such thing as

boring mathematics."

– EDSGER DIJKSTRA, computer scientist

DAY 95

The Maths Corner Habit

You have just looked at setting up a maths treasure basket to give your baby a fresh surprise each day and to ensure he or she is not overwhelmed and distracted by too many options.

Now, you are being introduced to the idea of a corner filled with maths toys and activities—which seems quite contradictory. However, both have their place in teaching your baby maths. The maths corner is a cosy haven where the two of you take time together, and you have number books, simple toys, and puzzles close to hand.

This corner is as much for you as it is for your baby. Some days, time passes extremely quickly. In the few spare minutes you might spend reading or doing a puzzle with your baby, you don't have a book nearby and the puzzle has its pieces spread all over the house. It is all too easy to give up before you have even begun. As a result, precious maths time with your baby disappears.

A maths corner allows you to have everything in one place. When your baby starts to crawl, it becomes a place to move *to*, thus signalling a desire to have special time with you.

Your cosy maths corner should be placed in a quiet area of your house but not too tucked away so you never sit there. It should offer a feeling of being sheltered and undisturbed while still being accessible. It could have only a beanbag or big cushion on the floor, plus a pile of books and a box of toys. However, for extra touches, consider these five suggestions.

1. Canopy, Netting, Hanging Material, Tent

Babies, toddlers, and children of all ages love the idea of dens, tents, and cosy places. If you opt for hanging material, you can change it to fit certain activities or stories you have in mind for that day.

2. Beanbags, Cushions, Comfy Chair

Any form of soft seating will be great. Low options such as floor cushions or beanbags can be ideal for your baby to snuggle up on. A rocking chair or oversized armchair provides a comfortable place that enables you to relax with your baby for some time.

3. Mirrors

Babies love mirrors. They are drawn to the shininess and love seeing another baby appear. Mirrors can be used for showing babies their reflections and counting their eyes, ears, mouth, and nose. When you add mirrors to your cosy corner, you provide a fun distraction for your baby.

4. Sensory Lighting

It is a lovely touch to change the atmosphere in the maths corner by adding lighting. You could have lights that allow you to select the colour, lamps that can be dimmed as bedtime approaches, star projectors, fish bubble tubes, or fairy lights. Any or all of these options will add to the magic of maths time.

5. Cuddly Toys and Blankets

You want this to be a welcoming place that your baby comes back to time and time again. You also want it to be a place to settle in and snuggle with you for as long as your baby is content. Adding a few blankets and soft cuddly toys will make it even more inviting.

►ACTIVITY◄

Make a maths corner

Find a suitable place with no phones and distractions to begin converting a basic space into the most welcoming corner of your house. Make it a place for you and your baby to bond and learn together. Let your baby see what you are doing and understand how special this together time is to you. If you get invested and excited about the maths corner, then your baby will, too.

★ ★ ★ ★ ★ ★ ★

What could be better than a cosy den with enchanting lighting containing a vast array of toys and books for your baby to explore?
Teaching your baby maths in this environment can be a magical, bonding experience for both of you.

DAY 96

What to put in the Maths Corner

You have this wonderfully tranquil, nurturing place to spend quality time with your baby. What should you have close to hand and include in your maths corner? Here are five suggestions to get you started.

1. Books

Always have a selection of books in your maths corner. If possible, include a variety of number or shape picture books, story books to demonstrate sequencing, lift-the-flap, and interactive books to get the maths talk flowing. If you can, schedule a weekly trip to your local library, ideally when it hosts story time or rhyme time. There, you can enjoy being part of an engaging baby's group and then select a few books to share in the days that follow. The novelty of exploring new stories and pictures encourages your baby to seek out the maths corner to explore what is there. It is also beneficial to have a few much-read, much-loved story books nearby.

Babies know what to expect in a place like a maths corner, which makes them feel safe. Reading the same book repeatedly also develops their logic skills. In effect, they are rehearsing their ability to predict events based on existing knowledge. For example, if you were to read your baby *The Monster at the End of This Book* by Jon Stone, babies who have heard the story several times will anticipate that the narrator is the monster—that is, they "predict" an outcome. Before long, they will use their awareness of patterns to make assertions about other things within the world of maths.

2. Toys

As discussed on DAY 38, several great toys can help your baby explore maths at his or her own pace. Placing toys in the maths corner will allow your baby to have unstructured time to learn through play. Chunky puzzles, building blocks, stacking toys, an activity cube, or slotting toys are ideal.

3. Musical Instruments

A small box of toys that make a noise can be a great addition to your maths corner. Rattles, bells, rain makers, shakers—anything your baby can grab and move around to experience the joy of making noise. Remember, music and maths go hand in hand.

4. Finger Puppets

Finger puppets and small cuddly toys can prove to be a great investment. For example, you can use them to add interest to stories or nursery rhymes. You can give them voices and play with them creatively to capture your baby's interest. When reciting a nursery rhyme such as 'Incy Wincy Spider' if you are teaching the mathematical word of "up", then having a spider for your baby to watch going *up* makes that word real and easier to learn and understand. If you have a glove puppet with five little ducks, one for each finger, then your baby will be mesmerised as the number of ducks decrease and then suddenly come back at the end. These simple props help keep your baby's interest and make maths time extra fun.

5. Treasure Basket

Having toys that will be accessible consistently is reassuring for babies. It gives them time to develop and grow their play with these items. However, novelty is exciting and stimulating for your baby, especially when it is within a safe environment. So, placing your treasure box or basket in the maths corner and having something new and interesting for your baby to interact with, ideally daily, works well.

Your maths corner should be a wonderful place full of love, comfort, and fun. These ingredients are essential for your baby to be in a positive mindset and absorb new ideas.

▶ ACTIVITY ◀

Make a spider with your baby

1. Start by letting your baby paint a piece of paper black. You can supply a brush but do not be surprised if he or she ends up rubbing on paint with their hands.

2. While that paper is drying, cut out eight legs. These could be pieces of string or black wool or just strips of black paper.

3. When the painted paper is dry, scrunch it into a ball, pointing out to your baby that it was a **flat rectangle** that has become a **sphere**. Then stick on the eight legs, counting them as you go.

4. Add eyes, either from white paper or craft eyes. Talk about there being **two circular** eyes.

5. With your spider finished, it is time to sing 'Incy, Wincy Spider' to your baby. Use your paper spider to emphasise the mathematical word "up" and your fingers as rain for "down".

Books, toys, instruments, and puppets—everything you need in one tranquil, nurturing place.
What better way to teach your baby maths!

16

MATHS HABIT 5 - FOCUS TIME

"Togetherness has to do with focused attention. It is giving someone your undivided attention. As humans, we have a fundamental desire to connect with others. We may be in the presence of people all day long, but we do not always feel connected."

– GARY CHAPMAN,
author, *5 Love Languages*

DAY 97

The Focus Time Habit

This is a lovely all-encompassing habit to end this book with. Consider it to be a habit to facilitate all the other habits—the important 'U' for Undivided Attention in N**U**MBER TALK.

It can be hard to find time during these crazy, busy, precious, fleeting years. The idea of managing to teach your baby maths on top of everything else could feel overwhelming and unachievable. That is where this comes in—the habit of giving your baby a few minutes of focused one-to-one time every day.

You may not realise how often your attention is divided as you juggle your baby, job, chores, and friendships every day. You may believe that, in this fast-paced world, multitasking is the most efficient (or only) way to get everything done. But psychologists would disagree.

Rather than being a solution, multitasking represents a problem for your brain. Flitting from one task to another slows you down and makes it hard to do everything to the best of your abilities.

And as harmful as multitasking can be for the brain, it also takes a toll on family relationships. If you are constantly checking emails and messages, or you're distracted by your never-ending "to do" list, then you are not interacting with your baby in a meaningful way.

Babies who spend less time interacting with their parents learn less by example than those with parents who are proactively involved.

Your baby needs you. Your baby needs your attention. Wonderfully, when the need for bonding, connection, and attention is met, your baby gains patience, begins to self-regulate, and is more open to learning than ever.

Inevitably, you have chores to do and calls to make throughout the day. But carve out as much time as possible to connect—just you and your baby. The concept of a few minutes focused time is simple yet astonishingly effective. Be realistic and manage your expectations, for focused time does not have to be perfect every day. Be flexible and persevere.

As with any habit, you need to believe it works. It may not ring true that just a few minutes can make a difference, but it definitely can. You have to try it to believe it!

You might find those focused minutes as rewarding as your baby does. You might even choose to focus on various things for a longer time, such as five minutes looking at a book full of patterns, five minutes dancing whilst counting the beat, five minutes looking at each other and chatting. But be realistic and know that a few minutes of your *full attention* each day is worth a lot.

When you get in from work or another commitment, it can take time to ease back into being a fully focused parent. If you can be consistent with your attention, though, your baby soon learns to await that special time coming up. It is important that, when you are ready to fully connect, you make it obvious: turn off the TV, shut down your laptop, and leave your phone in a different room.

You will learn new things in these focused times you might not have noticed before. You will learn more from interacting with your baby—discovering particular likes and dislikes—than you could ever learn from a book.

While forming this habit, you may need suggestions on how to spend the time initially. But before long, you will understand each other's needs and desires as you fall naturally into this special bonding time.

►ACTIVITY◄

Be fully present with your baby

The structure of reading a book, singing a rhyme, or giving a massage can help fill the one-to-one time you spend with your baby. However, on occasion, you might inadvertently rush through the activity and may not fully focus on your baby during the process.

Instead, be *present* and *bond*.

Today, remove all distractions and hold your baby close. Do your best to put all other thoughts out of your mind. Use this calm, quiet time to be mindful and meditate with your baby. He or she will channel your moods and rhythms as you count your breaths in and out. Notice your baby's body language and facial expression. Then mimic your baby's actions to acknowledge his or her contribution to this shared moment. Go at your baby's pace and learn.

The concept of spending a few minutes of
focused time is simple yet effective.
Those precious few minutes of your full
attention each day is worth a lot.
You have to try it to believe it!

DAY 98

How to Spend Your Focused Time

These six suggestions will ensure you are getting the most out of the focused time with your baby. Several will seem familiar because all previous habits can and should fall neatly into this category.

1. Conversation

The evidence is strong that conversations with babies are most effective when you are fully focused on them. Set aside a few minutes to hold your baby and listen to any vocalisations. Repeat those noises and take turns to "talk" and communicate. As the maths vocabulary flows, make sure your baby feels you value what he or she has to say. Use the power of the patterns involved in turn-taking to reinforce that you are listening and fully focused on the sounds your baby makes in response to your NUMBER TALK.

2. Stories

What a perfect way to invest a few minutes! As mentioned before, stories give a structure to your precious time together. They are both enjoyable and beneficial. You could count the pictures in a book, make up a tale with a sequence of events, or read your baby's favourite book to reinforce key concepts through repetition. Five minutes of storytelling is never a waste of time.

Reading during your special focus time gives you a chance to watch your baby's reactions to the pictures and words. When does he or she giggle? Are books with texture preferred? What about three-dimensional books? This is your baby's special time, so let him or her choose the book and the pace.

Reading before bedtime is a wonderful habit to get into, but it can become rushed. On occasion, you might find yourself galloping through the book before taking off to eat your dinner or get another child to bed. Instead, choose an additional five-minute slot where there is no agenda other than relaxing together. That's when you have an opportunity to completely focus on what your baby enjoys at that given time. You may only look at one page of a book in this time. Let your baby take the lead and set the pace.

3. Songs

Every parent has an experience of whizzing through a night-time lullaby and turning the light off as if to will the baby to fall fast asleep. The focus is not on the lovely song and the tender moment; it is on the goal of having a no-drama bedtime routine.

Every parent also has the experience of jiggling their baby and humming his or her favourite song for hours to get settled, knowing the song is the only thing to keep him or her calm.

Both of those experiences serve a purpose. However, another way to share a song is during the focused bonding time. Then the joy of the song and the moment becomes the focus, not a way to distract or cheer up or calm down your baby. Only to enjoy and bond!

You can take this time to experiment with different genres, pop songs, nursery rhymes, classical music. You can stop and start. You can certainly enjoy the moment. If, when singing 'The Wheels on the Bus', your baby is loving the verse where the babies on the bus go up and down, then repeat it and continue whooshing him or her "up" and "down" as you sing. Follow your baby's lead. You may realise you have made the maths elements of the song so fun, he or she wants more!

4. Outdoors

It is generally understood that babies need food, warmth, love, sleep, and fresh air to thrive. So, what better way to enjoy time with your baby than taking a few minutes to walk outside, play outside, or just sit and be outside.

With much to see and experience outdoors, often simply the feeling of space can entertain your baby. Okay, British weather is not always warm and pleasant. But don't forget that in Finland babies often sleep outside even in sub-zero temperatures. The point is, when dressed appropriately, babies enjoy the great outdoors come rain or shine—as long as they are with you.

How can you teach your baby maths while enjoying freedom and fresh air? You could: collect, sort, and count leaves, twigs, stones, and flowers; compare heights of trees or plants; play in the sandpit and explore the maths concepts of full and empty. Where is your baby happiest outdoors today? Where is your baby looking? What is your baby's focus? This is where your maths exploration should begin.

5. Games

A few minutes is the ideal amount of time for a quick game of peek-a-boo, this little piggy, tickling games, horsey rides on your lap, or bubble blowing and popping.

Remember, repetition is important. Do not be surprised if the first time you play peek-a-boo, your baby goes quiet with shock rather than giggling with glee. Many games will not work the first time you play them. However, babies love to know what is coming next. It will not be long before they are initiating the games and enjoying every minute.

Your baby has a lot of needs in the early days: a need to be fed, a need for sleep, a need for quiet time, a need for a clean nappy. Your baby's attention span varies a lot. You will know your baby is loving the game when he or she turns towards you smiling or laughing. But pay attention. If your baby squirms away from you, looks around, or cries, it is time to change the activity.

During focus time, there is no set end goal. If during a game your baby gets distracted, do not be tempted to complete the game. Simply watch and let him or her guide you.

6. Sensory Play

In truth, every aspect of your baby's play is sensory play. He or she is exploring with all five senses while learning and developing all the time. However, a few minutes of preparation will help make your focused sensory play time all the more enjoyable and relaxed.

Use what you have at home and let your child explore with you. Ideas include:

- moulding shaving foam or sculpting sand into 3D shapes
- squeezing sponges and watching them reform, going from smaller to bigger
- ripping Velcro apart, revealing a rough and a smooth side
- exploring food fun with rice and spaghetti, dry and cooked, to compare and contrast

By stimulating babies' senses, you help them develop not only cognitively but also creatively, socially, emotionally, linguistically and physically—simply by playing with them.

►ACTIVITY◄

Brush your baby's skin

A lovely bonding activity you can do with undivided attention is to gently brush your baby's arms and legs with a soft brush (e.g., a paint brush or a baby hairbrush). Brush therapists use a soft scrubbing brush.

Brushing skin is a therapeutic technique that might help with autism, attention deficit disorder, and sensory processing disorder. Brushing stimulates specific nerve endings, which enhances their development.

As you brush your baby's legs up or down, left or right, count the strokes while talking and using the language of maths.

As a bonus, brushing helps calm your baby and gives the two of you one-to-one time to be fully together in the moment.

★ ★ ★ ★ ★ ★ ★

Every maths activity in this book lends itself
to being a focus-time activity. But be realistic.
Take each day and each activity as it comes.
Don't worry if, on occasion, you whizz through a
song while checking emails and cooking dinner.
Just try again tomorrow.

17

CONCLUSION

"The only way to learn mathematics

is to do mathematics."

– PAUL HALMOS,
mathematical expositor

DAY 99

The Importance of Parental Expectations

You may have heard of the Pygmalion effect, a psychological occurrence in which high expectations lead to improved performance and high achievement.

In their 1968 book *Pygmalion in the Classroom,* Robert Rosenthal and Leonare Jacobson looked at this phenomenon in practice and told teachers that certain pupils had the potential to become high achievers. The pupils they had selected were, in fact, randomly picked. However, by the end of the year, the chosen pupils did indeed progress more than those not selected.

This highlights the influence of self-fulfilling prophecies, defined as "a false definition of the situation evoking a behaviour that makes the originally false conception come true". In essence, that means your expectations will influence yours and your baby's actions and beliefs. If you think your baby will struggle with learning maths, then you make this outcome more likely. If you believe maths is fun and achievable for your baby, then your expectation will have a positive influence on your baby's maths confidence, educational attainment, and enjoyment.

Parental involvement and expectations matter. It is something that you can, and absolutely should, act on as soon as possible. Your baby is definitely not too young to be told that he or she can succeed at learning maths.

From a meta-analysis of studies, it has been shown that parental expectations have nearly twice the effect on children's achievement as parenting style (e.g., providing a supportive home environment with adequate discipline). That is not to say you shouldn't have a supportive home and good boundaries. Just know that parents' expectations of their babies will set the babies' expectations of themselves.

It seems unbelievably simple that expecting your baby to enjoy and be good at maths will mean it actually happens. But it is true! Your involvement and expectations are key to your children achieving their potential.

Babies use their impressive understanding of maths already every day. And their need for maths knowledge will only increase as the years pass. So, believe in your baby and help him or her believe too.

►ACTIVITY◄

See maths everywhere

No one game or activity will teach your baby maths. The secret is realising that maths is everywhere—in everything your baby does and sees.

Today and going forward, look for the maths in all inter-actions and embrace it. This might involve emphasising a maths word in a book or a nursery rhyme, pointing out shapes as you walk outside, discussing positions your baby moves into when rolling or crawling—you get the picture.

If you believe maths is everywhere and know your baby will benefit from you pointing it out, then your expectations about teaching your baby maths will come true!

Your expectations of your baby's maths ability are important.
Convey to your baby you *believe* that he or she can enjoy and succeed in maths.

DAY 100

Final Thoughts

There should be no doubt in your mind that teaching your baby maths is good. It is amazing that simply using number words every day will most likely increase your baby's maths ability upon entry to school. And having maths knowledge when starting school is a bigger predictor of later academic achievement than reading or social skills.

This book has not only set out to give you ways to introduce maths to your baby via simple, fun activities. Its purpose is to highlight the following facts:

1. Babies seem to be born with an amazing number sense: understanding shapes in the womb, being aware of quantities at seven hours old, assessing probability at six months old, and comprehending addition and subtraction at nine months old.

2. The best time to introduce maths is infancy. By the time children enter school, there is already a significant gap in maths skills.

3. A parent's attitude shapes a child's attitude. You have the power to teach your baby that maths is enjoyable and not something to be anxious about.

4. Your baby can learn maths while boosting all other areas of development. For example, movement will be boosted

while teaching geometry positional language, literacy will be boosted while reading a "number" book, and bonding will be boosted while giving your baby your undivided attention teaching maths to him or her.

5. Babies will use maths every day for the rest of their lives. That's why maths is important.

There is no downside to teaching your baby maths!

▶ACTIVITY◀

Plan the next week's maths activities

Get into the habit of thinking about how to bring maths into your baby's life every day. Refill your treasure basket and restock your pile of books, so you're ready to keep your baby's maths journey going.

★ ★ ★ ★ ★ ★ ★

**Enjoy exploring maths with your baby
today and every day!**

REFERENCES

DAY 1

1. A New Approach to Making the UK Numerate,
Nationalnumeracy.org.uk

2. Izard V, Sann C, Spelke ES, Streri A (2009). Newborn infants
perceive abstract numbers *PNAS,* June 23, 2009. 106 (25) 10382-
10385.

DAY 2

3. Levine S, Suriyakham L, Rowe M, Huttenlocher J, Gunderson E.
(2010). What Counts in the Development of Young Children's
Number Knowledge? *Developmental Psychology.* 46. 1309-19.

DAY 3

4. Duncan GJ, Dowsett CJ, Claessens A, Magnuson K, Huston AC,
Klebanov P, Pagani LS, Feinstein L, Engel M, Brooks-Gunn J, Sexton
H, Duckworth K, Japel C. School readiness and later achievement.
Dev Psychol. 2007 Nov;43(6):1428-1446.

DAY 6

5. Ivy AS, Brunson KL, Sandman C, Baram TZ. Dysfunctional
nurturing behavior in rat dams with limited access to nesting
material: a clinically relevant model for early-life stress.
Neuroscience. 2008 Jun 26;154(3):1132-42.

DAY 11

6. Gratier M, Devouche E, Guellai B, Infanti R, Yilmaz E, Parlato-Oliveira E. (2015). Early development of turn-taking in vocal interaction between mothers and infants. *Frontiers in Psychology, 6, Article 1167.*

7. Romeo RR, Segaran J, Leonard JA, Robinson ST, West MR, Mackey AP, Yendiki A, Rowe ML, Gabrieli JDE. (2018). Language Exposure Relates to Structural Neural Connectivity in Childhood. *The Journal of Neuroscience.* 38(36):7870-7877.

DAY 12

8. Doherty-Sneddon G (2008). The great baby signing debate: academia meets public interest. Psychologist. 21.

DAY 15

9. Bergelson E, Swingley D (2012). At 6–9 months, human infants know the meanings of many common nouns. Proceedings of the National Academy of Sciences of the United States of America. 109. 3253-8.

DAY 16

10. Durkin K, Shire B, Riem R, Crowther R, Rutter D. (2011). The social and linguistic context of early number use. *British Journal of Developmental Psychology.* 4. 269-288.

DAY 20 & 22

11. Gunderson EA, Levine SC. Some types of parent number talk count more than others: relations between parents' input and children's cardinal-number knowledge. (2011) *Developmental Science.* 14(5):1021-1032.

DAY 24

12. Xu F, Garcia V. Intuitive statistics by 8-month-old infants. (2008). Proceedings of the National Academy of Sciences. 105 (13) 5012-5015

DAY 31

13. Berger A, Tzur G, Posner MI. (2006). Infant brains detect arithmetic errors. *Proceedings of the National Academy of Sciences* USA. 103(33):12649-53.

14. McCrink K, Wynn K. (2004). Large-Number Addition and Subtraction by 9-Month-Old Infants. *Psychological Science, 15*(11), 776-781.

DAY 32

15. Reid VM, Dunn K, Young RJ, Amu J, Donovan T, Reissland N. The Human Fetus Preferentially Engages with Face-like Visual Stimuli. (2017). *Current Biology.* 27(12):1825-1828.

DAY 34

16. Ferguson B, Franconeri S, Waxman S. (2018). Very young infants learn abstract rules in the visual modality. *PLoS One.* 13.

DAY 35

17. Althaus N, Plunkett K. (2016). Categorization in infancy: labelling induces a persisting focus on commonalities. *Developmental Science*, 19(5), 770–80.

DAY 36

18. Thomsen L. (2011). Infants ascribe social dominance to larger individuals. Harvard University.

DAY 37

19. Fitzgerald HE, Lintz LM, Brackbill Y, Adams G. (1967). Time perception and conditioning an autonomic response in human infants. *Perceptual and Motor Skills*. 24(2):479-86.

DAY 43

20. www.inpp.org.uk

DAY 58

21. Chang A, Sandhofer CM, Brown CS. (2011). Gender Biases in Early Number Exposure to Preschool-Aged Children. *Journal of Language and Social Psychology*. 30(4):440-450.

DAY 60

22. https://www.youcubed.org/wp-content/uploads/2017/04/JACmaths-seeing-article.pdf

DAY 65

23. Serçe H. (2009). Using Popular Songs to Teach Vocabulary.

DAY 66

24. Rauscher FH, Shaw GL, Ky KN. (1993). Music and spatial task performance. *Nature 365* 611.

DAY 67

25. Zeedyk MS. (2008). What's life in a baby buggy like? The impact of buggy orientation on parent-infant interaction and infant stress. In collaboration with the National Literacy Trust www.literacytrust.org.uk

DAY 68

26. Zimmerman FJ, Christakis DA, Meltzoff AN. (2007). Television and DVD/video viewing in children younger than 2 years. *Archives of Pediatrics and Adolescent Medicine.* 161(5):473-9.

27. DeLoache JS, Chiong C, Sherman K, Islam N, Vanderborght M, Troseth GL, Strouse GA, O'Doherty K. (2010). Do babies learn from baby media? *Psychological Science.* 21(11):1570-4.

DAY 69

28. Programme for International Student Assessment (PISA) www.oecd.org

DAY 70

29. Bath SC, Steer CD, Golding J, Emmett P, Rayman MP. (2013). Effect of inadequate iodine status in UK pregnant women on cognitive outcomes in their children: results from the Avon Longitudinal Study of Parents and Children (ALSPAC). *Lancet* 382(9889):331-7.

DAY 71

30. Seehagen S, Konrad C, Herbert J S, Schneider S. (2015). Timely sleep facilitates declarative memory consolidation in infants. *Proceedings of the National Academy of Sciences* USA. 112(5):1625-9.

DAY 72

31. Wolfgang C, Stannard L, Jones I. (2003). Advanced constructional play with LEGOs among preschoolers as a

predictor of later school achievement in mathematics. *Early Child Development and Care.* 173. 467-475.

DAY 73

32. Dweck CS, Yeager DS. (2019). Mindsets: A View From Two Eras. *Perspectives on Psychological Science,* vol. 14, no. 3, 481–496.

DAY 75

33. The 2011 Skills for Life Survey: A Survey of Literacy, Numeracy and ICT Levels in England Ref: BIS/12/P168. December 2012

34. The impact of poor numeracy skills on adults. Prepared for NIACE by the National Research and Development Centre for Adult Literacy and Numeracy (NRDC) at the Institute of Education (IOE). June 2013

35. Carpentieri JD, Lister J, Frumkin L. (2009). Adult numeracy: a review of research. National Research and Development Centre for Adult Literacy and Numeracy.

DAY 76

36. Lally P, Jaarsveld C, Potts H, Wardle J. (2009). How are habits formed: Modeling habit formation in the real world. *European Journal of Social Psychology.* 40.

DAY 79

37. Hart B, Risley T. (2016). *The Early Catastrophe: The 30 Million Word Gap by Age 3.* 1st ed. Baltimore, MD: Brookes Publishing 4-9.

DAY 80

38. Fernald A, Marchman VA, Weisleder A. (2013). SES differences in language processing skill and vocabulary are evident at 18 months. *Developmental Science*. 16(2):234-248.

DAY 81

39. Ramírez-Esparza N, Garcia-Sierra A, Kuhl P. (2014). Look who's talking: Speech style and social context in language input to infants are linked to concurrent and future speech development. *Developmental Science*. 17.

DAY 82

40. Jimenez M, Mendelsohn A, Lin Y, Shelton P, Reichman N. (2019). Early Shared Reading Is Associated with Less Harsh Parenting. *Journal of Developmental & Behavioral Pediatrics*. 40.

DAY 83

41. Protzko J, Aronson J, Blair C. (2013). How to Make a Young Child Smarter: Evidence From the Database of Raising Intelligence. *Perspectives on Psychological Science*. 8(1):25-40.

INDEX

creativity, 186

gender bias, 178-181

"maths gene," 175-176

rote learning and repetition, 182

N

naming, 18-20, 152

napping, 219

National Curriculum

Key Stage 1, 89-90

time, topic of, 112

National Literacy Trust, 207

neuroscience, 184

newborns, and sleep, 219

newborns, studies on numeracy skills of, 3-4

nouns, key words, 251

novelty, 226

number skills, 91

NUMBER TALK, 15-47, 152, 181

number words. see also counting; sets of objects

exposure to, 6-7, 8

number walks, 84

nursery rhymes, 120

nursery rhymes. see also songs

curriculum, 166-167

NUMBER TALK, 38-40

number words, 120, 171

positional words, 100, 257

sleep routine, 220

nutrition. see diet

O

object permanence, 223

obstacle course, 101, 131

obstacles, dealing with, 243-245

omega-3 oils, 216-217

"one," 154

one-to-one maths time, 143. see also focus time

ordering, 91, 102, 106-107

outdoors, 322

P

paper ripping, 127

parental attention, 21-23, 149, 210-211, 271

parentese, 255-257

patterns, 102-104. see also sequences

and interacting with your baby, 23

and maths, 186

in play, 86, 90

rhymes and music, 38, 120, 150, 202

stories/books, 312

and symmetry, 104, 187

peek-a-boo, 34, 282, 323

personal, social, and emotional development, 137, 141-142

phonemes. see sounds and phonemes

physical development, 138. see also actions; movement

play. see also craft; music; toys, for maths; treasure basket

balloons, 119

bath fun, 91

geometry, 90, 91

hide and seek, 62

interactive/baby-led, 183, 280

money/shops, 234

play-doh, 246, 291

pretend libraries, 272

ACKNOWLEDGEMENTS

Writing a book has been harder than I thought, but more rewarding than I could have ever imagined. One thing is for sure: I certainly could not have achieved it on my own.

First and foremost, I would like to thank the many insanely clever people who invest their time and effort researching infant development. The more research papers I read, the more I was blown away by the depth and breadth of knowledge available— not to mention the impressively diverse ways these researchers devised to assess the skills of mini-humans who cannot yet talk or walk. I extend my personal thanks to John Protzko, Suzanne Zeedyk, Fred Zimmerman, Vincent Reid, Catherine Sandhofer, Alicia Chang, Véronique Izard, Tallie Baram, Phillippa Lally, Elika Bergelson, Hüseyin Serçe, Liz Gunderson, Nairán Ramirez-Esparza, Fei Xu, Koleen McCrink, Andrea Berger, Nadja Althaus, and Jo Boaler. All of these people kindly contributed their thoughts when I reached out to them. Thank you.

Next, I express my gratitude to Barbara McNichol, a true expert in her field of editing non-fiction writing. I won't lie; when the sample edit came back mainly red with amendments on virtually every line, I felt less sure of my ability to write. However, I am so pleased I put my trust in her. I am especially grateful for the detail and speed with which she rewrote parts of my manuscript. Thank you, Barbara. You absolutely delivered on your promise to preserve my voice while adding clarity.

I started drafting this book after reading an article Tony Attwood had written about dyscalculia. I never for one minute thought he would agree to write the foreword, but it turns out there really is no harm in asking. Thank you, Tony!

Before starting this project, I had never heard of "Beta Readers", but I am glad the existence of such kind, generous individuals came onto my radar. I was so excited when I discovered that people might be willing to read my manuscript—for free! I tentatively put a post on Facebook and sat back expecting tumbleweed to roll by (I was aware infant mathematics is a relatively niche area). I could not have been more wrong. I received hundreds of comments—admittedly some not completely enthusiastic about the premise—and plenty of beta readers willing to read as much as they could in one week. Wow! The feedback was amazingly constructive and useful. Particular thanks to Leslie, Samantha, Amy, and Lewa who gave me detailed pointers to improve my content and structure. An extra special thanks to Alexandria who found time to read and critique this book while looking after her two-month-old baby. Thank you!

Now for my closer-to-home acknowledgements. Though I did not mention my new book-writing hobby to many people, those I confided in helped me more than I can justify. From cover choices to grammar checks, I received instant help, advice, and support. I consider myself incredibly lucky to have friends like Katharine, Dawn, and Jenny. The next year of brunches are on me!

All good marriages deal with constant compromises. When I chose to indulge my urge to write this book, it inevitably led to my already over-worked husband making even more compromises than normal. From reading early drafts—even being brave enough to voice critiques—to walking the dog, cooking Sunday roast, and going climbing with our children so I could steal small pockets of time to write in peace. My husband's support and belief in me made all the difference. Thank you, Rich, I'm very lucky to have you by my side on all our adventures together.

Finally, my inspiration and my confirmation are my amazing children, Henry and Isla. You have kept me going by laughing when I used the Word "Read Aloud" function and we listened to my manuscript being read in the most monotone voice, and by banning me from talking about food fractions now you're both bona fide maths masters. I will never be able to stop telling you how proud I am of all you have both achieved and how much I love you! I have enjoyed writing this book, but the best job I could ever have is being your mum. Thank you both for being so uniquely, perfectly you!

ABOUT THE AUTHOR

Emma Smith is a fellow of The Institute of Actuaries and a chartered accountant. A double academic prize winner with a First-Class Maths degree, she is a lifelong lover of maths. Since having children, Emma has worked freelance as an actuarial exam counsellor, an assistant examiner, and writer, publishing such articles as "Your Baby is a Genius!" in *Baby London Magazine*.

Emma is ably assisted by her dog, Button, her daughter's cat, Princess Marshmallow, and her son's cat, Squeezy Paws.